LAYERS OF LEARNING
YEAR FOUR • UNIT SIXTEEN

VIETNAM WAR
ATLANTIC STATES
FOOD CHAINS
PHOTOGRAPHY

Published by HooDoo Publishing
United States of America
© 2017 Layers of Learning
(Grilled Cheese BTN Font) © Fontdiner - www.fontdiner.com
ISBN #978-1548957711

Units at a Glance: Topics For All Four Years of the Layers of Learning Program

1	History	Geography	Science	The Arts
1	Mesopotamia	Maps & Globes	Planets	Cave Paintings
2	Egypt	Map Keys	Stars	Egyptian Art
3	Europe	Global Grids	Earth & Moon	Crafts
4	Ancient Greece	Wonders	Satellites	Greek Art
5	Babylon	Mapping People	Humans in Space	Poetry
6	The Levant	Physical Earth	Laws of Motion	List Poems
7	Phoenicians	Oceans	Motion	Moral Stories
8	Assyrians	Deserts	Fluids	Rhythm
9	Persians	Arctic	Waves	Melody
10	Ancient China	Forests	Machines	Chinese Art
11	Early Japan	Mountains	States of Matter	Line & Shape
12	Arabia	Rivers & Lakes	Atoms	Color & Value
13	Ancient India	Grasslands	Elements	Texture & Form
14	Ancient Africa	Africa	Bonding	African Tales
15	First North Americans	North America	Salts	Creative Kids
16	Ancient South America	South America	Plants	South American Art
17	Celts	Europe	Flowering Plants	Jewelry
18	Roman Republic	Asia	Trees	Roman Art
19	Christianity	Australia & Oceania	Simple Plants	Instruments
20	Roman Empire	You Explore	Fungi	Composing Music

2	History	Geography	Science	The Arts
1	Byzantines	Turkey	Climate & Seasons	Byzantine Art
2	Barbarians	Ireland	Forecasting	Illumination
3	Islam	Arabian Peninsula	Clouds & Precipitation	Creative Kids
4	Vikings	Norway	Special Effects	Viking Art
5	Anglo Saxons	Britain	Wild Weather	King Arthur Tales
6	Charlemagne	France	Cells & DNA	Carolingian Art
7	Normans	Nigeria	Skeletons	Canterbury Tales
8	Feudal System	Germany	Muscles, Skin, Cardio	Gothic Art
9	Crusades	Balkans	Digestive & Senses	Religious Art
10	Burgundy, Venice, Spain	Switzerland	Nerves	Oil Paints
11	Wars of the Roses	Russia	Health	Minstrels & Plays
12	Eastern Europe	Hungary	Metals	Printmaking
13	African Kingdoms	Mali	Carbon Chemistry	Textiles
14	Asian Kingdoms	Southeast Asia	Non-metals	Vivid Language
15	Mongols	Caucasus	Gases	Fun With Poetry
16	Medieval China & Japan	China	Electricity	Asian Arts
17	Pacific Peoples	Micronesia	Circuits	Arts of the Islands
18	American Peoples	Canada	Technology	Indian Legends
19	The Renaissance	Italy	Magnetism	Renaissance Art I
20	Explorers	Caribbean Sea	Motors	Renaissance Art II

3	History	Geography	Science	The Arts
1	Age of Exploration	Argentina & Chile	Classification & Insects	Fairy Tales
2	The Ottoman Empire	Egypt & Libya	Reptiles & Amphibians	Poetry
3	Mogul Empire	Pakistan & Afghanistan	Fish	Mogul Arts
4	Reformation	Angola & Zambia	Birds	Reformation Art
5	Renaissance England	Tanzania & Kenya	Mammals & Primates	Shakespeare
6	Thirty Years' War	Spain	Sound	Baroque Music
7	The Dutch	Netherlands	Light & Optics	Baroque Art I
8	France	Indonesia	Bending Light	Baroque Art II
9	The Enlightenment	Korean Peninsula	Color	Art Journaling
10	Russia & Prussia	Central Asia	History of Science	Watercolors
11	Conquistadors	Baltic States	Igneous Rocks	Creative Kids
12	Settlers	Peru & Bolivia	Sedimentary Rocks	Native American Art
13	13 Colonies	Central America	Metamorphic Rocks	Settler Sayings
14	Slave Trade	Brazil	Gems & Minerals	Colonial Art
15	The South Pacific	Australasia	Fossils	Principles of Art
16	The British in India	India	Chemical Reactions	Classical Music
17	The Boston Tea Party	Japan	Reversible Reactions	Folk Music
18	Founding Fathers	Iran	Compounds & Solutions	Rococo
19	Declaring Independence	Samoa & Tonga	Oxidation & Reduction	Creative Crafts I
20	The American Revolution	South Africa	Acids & Bases	Creative Crafts II

4	History	Geography	Science	The Arts
1	American Government	USA	Heat & Temperature	Patriotic Music
2	Expanding Nation	Pacific States	Motors & Engines	Tall Tales
3	Industrial Revolution	U.S. Landscapes	Energy	Romantic Art I
4	Revolutions	Mountain West States	Energy Sources	Romantic Art II
5	Africa	U.S. Political Maps	Energy Conversion	Impressionism I
6	The West	Southwest States	Earth Structure	Impressionism II
7	Civil War	National Parks	Plate Tectonics	Post Impressionism
8	World War I	Plains States	Earthquakes	Expressionism
9	Totalitarianism	U.S. Economics	Volcanoes	Abstract Art
10	Great Depression	Heartland States	Mountain Building	Kinds of Art
11	World War II	Symbols & Landmarks	Chemistry of Air & Water	War Art
12	Modern East Asia	The South	Food Chemistry	Modern Art
13	India's Independence	People of America	Industry	Pop Art
14	Israel	Appalachian States	Chemistry of Farming	Modern Music
15	Cold War	U.S. Territories	Chemistry of Medicine	Free Verse
16	Vietnam War	Atlantic States	Food Chains	Photography
17	Latin America	New England States	Animal Groups	Latin American Art
18	Civil Rights	Home State Study I	Instincts	Theater & Film
19	Technology	Home State Study II	Habitats	Architecture
20	Terrorism	America in Review	Conservation	Creative Kids

Unit 4-16

Printable Pack

This unit includes printables at the end. To make life easier for you we also created digital printable packs for each unit. To retrieve your printable pack for Unit 4-16, please visit

www.layers-of-learning.com/digital-printable-packs/

Put the printable pack in your shopping cart and use this coupon code:

7117UNIT4-16

Your printable pack will be free.

Layers of Learning Introduction

This is part of a series of units in the Layers of Learning homeschool curriculum, including the subjects of history, geography, science, and the arts. Children from 1st through 12th can participate in the same curriculum at the same time - family school style.

The units are intended to be used in order as the basis of a complete curriculum (once you add in a systematic math, reading, and writing program). You begin with Year 1 Unit 1 no matter what ages your children are. Spend about 2 weeks on each unit. You pick and choose the activities within the unit that appeal to you and read the books from the book list that are available to you or find others on the same topic from your library. We highly recommend that you use the timeline in every history section as the backbone. Then flesh out your learning with reading and activities that highlight the topics you think are the most important.

Alternatively, you can use the units as activity ideas to supplement another curriculum in any order you wish. You can still use them with all ages of children at the same time.

When you've finished with Year One, move on to Year Two, Year Three, and Year Four. Then begin again with Year One and work your way through the years again. Now your children will be older, reading more involved books, and writing more in depth. When you have completed the sequence for the second time, you start again on it for the third and final time. If your student began with Layers of Learning in 1st grade and stayed with it all the way through she would go through the four year rotation three times, firmly cementing the information in her mind in ever increasing depth. At each level you should expect increasing amounts of outside reading and writing. High schoolers in particular should be reading extensively, and if possible, participating in discussion groups.

These icons will guide you in spotting activities and books that are appropriate for the age of child you are working with. But if you think an activity is too juvenile or too difficult for your kids, adjust accordingly. The icons are not there as rules, just guides.

🙂 1st-4th
🙂 5th-8th
🙂 9th-12th

Within each unit we share:

EXPLORATIONS, activities relating to the topic;
EXPERIMENTS, usually associated with science topics;
EXPEDITIONS, field trips;
EXPLANATIONS, teacher helps or educational philosophies.

In the sidebars we also include Additional Layers, Famous Folks, Fabulous Facts, On the Web, and other extra related topics that can take you off on tangents, exploring the world and your interests with a bit more freedom. The curriculum will always be there to pull you back on track when you're ready.

UNIT SIXTEEN
VIETNAM WAR - ATLANTIC STATES - FOOD CHAINS - PHOTOGRAPHY

Fairy tales are more than true: not because they tell us that dragons exist, but because they tell us that dragons can be beaten.
-Neil Gaiman, English author

LIBRARY LIST

HISTORY	Search for: Vietnam War , war protests
	😊 The Wall by Eve Bunting. A young child and his father visit the Vietnam War Memorial and search for Grandpa's name. A great jumping off place for a discussion.
	😊 Year of the Jungle by Suzanne Collins. An autobiographical picture book of a young girl's father going away to war in Vietnam.
	😊 Patrol: An American Soldier in Vietnam by Walter Dean Meyers.
	😊 😊 Vietnam War POWs by Danielle Smith-Llera.
	😊 😊 Jungle Scout: A Vietnam War Story by Tim Hoppey. Graphic novel.
	😊 😊 Inside Out and Back Again by Thanhha Lai. A young girl and her family must flee Saigon during the Vietnam War.
	😊 The Vietnam War by Paul Dowswell. Goes into the history and the causes.
	😊 The Vietnam War from KidCaps.
	😊 Cracker! The Best Dog in Vietnam by Cynthia Kadohata.
	😊 Fighting the Vietnam War by Brian Fitzgerald.
	😊 Goodbye, Vietnam by Gloria Wheelan. A Vietnamese family escapes the war as refugees and flees to Hong Kong and then to America.
	😊 The Land I Lost: Adventures of a Boy in Vietnam by Quang Nhuong Huynh. True stories of the author's boyhood in a peaceful rural Vietnam before the war.
	😊 The Vietnam War: An Interactive Modern History Adventure by Michael Burgan.
	😊 Vehicles of the Vietnam War by Michelle Levine.
	😊 😊 Vietnam War from DK.
	😊 😊 10,000 Days of Thunder: A History of the Vietnam War by Philip Caputo. The author actually fought in Vietnam and tells of his experiences plus explains the origins of the war and why he thinks America lost. Lots of pictures and maps.
	😊 😊 I Pledge Allegiance by Chris Lynch. This is the first in a novelized series about Vietnam. It has intense scenes and mild bad language. Parents should pre-read.
	😊 😊 The Journal Of Patrick Seamus Flaherty, United States Marine Corps by Ellen White. Intense war scenes and some bad language. Parents should pre-read.
	😊 😊 Escape from Saigon: How a Vietnam War Orphan Became an American Boy by Andrea Warren.
	😊 Vietnam: No Regrets: One Soldier's "Tour of Duty" by J. Richard Watkins. Gritty and realistic true story. Parents should pre-read.

GEOGRAPHY	Search for: Delaware, Maryland, Pennsylvania, New York, New Jersey ☺ F is for First State: A Delaware Alphabet by Carol Crane. ☺ B is for Blue Crab: A Maryland Alphabet by Shirley C. Menendez. ☺ K Is for Keystone: A Pennsylvania Alphabet by Kristen Kane. ☺ This Is New York by Miroslav Sasek. ☺ E is for Empire: A New York Alphabet by Ann E. Burg. ☺ G is for Garden State: A New Jersey Alphabet by Eileen Cameron. ☺ ☻ The New Jersey Reader by Trinka Hakes Noble.
SCIENCE	Search for: food chains, food webs, ecology ☺ Who Eats What?: Food Chains and Food Web by Patricia Lauber. ☺ What If There Were No Gray Wolves?: A Book About the Temperate Forest Ecosystem by Suzanne Slade. Examines how important one species can be to the ecosystem. There are other titles in this series worth checking out. ☺ My First Book About Backyard Nature: Ecology for Kids! by Patricia J. Wynne. ☺ ☻ What Are Food Chains and Webs? by Bobbie Kalman. ☺ ☻ DK Eyewitness Books: Ecology by Brian Lane. ☺ ☻ Producers, Consumers, and Decomposers by Dava Pressberg. ☺ ☻ An Ocean Food Chain by A.D. Tarbox. Look for others in the series by the same author.
THE ARTS	Search for: photography, George Eastman, Edwin H. Land, Louis Daguerre, Steven Sasson, Ansel Adams, Mathew Brady, Anne Geddes, Annie Leibovitz ☺ ☻ Click! A Story About George Eastman by Barbara Mitchell. A simple biography about George Eastman, creator of Kodak. ☺ ☻ ☻ Matthew Brady: Civil War Photographer by Elizabeth Van Steenwyk. A biography of the famous American Civil War photographer. ☺ ☻ Go Photo! An Activity Book for Kids by Alice Proujansky. Simple, fun, and creative photography-inspired projects for kids. ☺ ☻ National Geographic Kids Guide to Photography: Tips & Tricks on How to Be a Great Photographer From the Pros & Your Pals at My Shot by Annie Griffiths and Nancy Honovich. Dovetails with many things that are discussed in this unit and talks about ways to become a more thoughtful photographer. ☺ ☻ ☻ Photography Demystified for Kids: A Kids Guide and Parents Resource for Fun and Learning Photography Together by David McKay. ☺ ☻ Maker Projects for Kids Who Love Photography by Kelly Spence. This book includes photography projects for those who are interested and want to delve deeper. ☺ ☻ Creative Photography Lab: 52 Fun Exercises for Developing Self-Expression with your Camera by Steve Sonheim and Carla Sonheim. This book also includes projects. ☺ ☻ A Beautiful Mess Photo Idea Book: 95 Inspiring Ideas for Photographing Your Friends, Your World, and Yourself by Elsie Larson and Emma Chapman. Includes tips and photo challenges.

History: Vietnam War

Additional Layer

U.S. President Dwight D. Eisenhower helped rig a corrupt election so that anti-communist Ngo Dihn Diem could take power in South Vietnam in 1955.

Meanwhile in the North, the communists won every election with 99% of the vote.

It can be argued that if Americans didn't fix elections in the South, the communists would have.

Do the ends justify the means? As long as the outcome is good, can you do *anything* to get there? Why or why not?

Additional Layer

In America it is known as the Vietnam War, but in other places it is known as the Second Indochina War. In Vietnam it is known as the American War.

Deep Thoughts

Read this article: http://www.nationalreview.com/article/293017/reflections-cambodia-douglas-b-levene. What are the fatal flaws of communism, and why has that philosophy always led to death?

The French owned the country of Vietnam from colonial days until World War II when the Japanese occupied it. At the end of WWII the French tried to reassert their domination but were met with resistance. The First Indochina War resulted in the independence of Vietnam in 1954, but the country immediately split into two factions, the communist North and the republican South. The North Vietnamese began to attack and infiltrate the South Vietnamese, and war began. At the time, the United States was very concerned about the spread of communism, and so the government very closely and carefully watched the progress of the war, giving aid and arms to the South Vietnamese. Meanwhile, the Chinese and Soviet communists were giving aid and arms to the North Vietnamese.

Civilians were frequently caught up in the fighting. This woman and her children are trying to flee with help from these U.S. soldiers. They have been pinned down by attacking Viet Cong.

In 1965, regular American troops were deployed to Vietnam for the first time. The U.S. strategy was to fight an air war, dropping bombs on major northern cities and along the Ho Chi Minh Trail, the main route south. More bombs were dropped on Vietnam than were dropped on Europe during World War II. But U.S. troop levels continued to escalate, and a lot of the fighting was done on the ground in hand to hand combat as well. Opposing the U.S. were the regular North Vietnamese Army, who fought conventionally with large battle formations in several engagements, and the Viet Cong, South Vietnamese guerrillas who were sympathetic to the North.

The Viet Cong were a formidable enemy, not because they were well-equipped or well-organized, but because they were and could be anybody. Rural farmers, factory workers, your laundry boy, a five-year-old peasant girl - any of these could be carrying explosives or toting a gun through the jungle. They also set booby traps along jungle trails. American troops could be attacked anywhere, anytime, and in the most unexpected ways. There were no front lines and there was no well-defined enemy.

In January of 1968, during the ceasefire of the Tet Lunar New Year Celebrations, the North Vietnamese and the Viet Cong launched their last major offensive. In spite of brutal losses for the Americans, the Viet Cong and the North Vietnamese army were completely outclassed by American firepower, technology, and manpower. They were desperate, and this was their last attempt. Hundreds of thousands of troops all over Vietnam simultaneously attacked on the first day of the ceasefire, surprising and driving back U.S. and South Vietnamese troops. But the lost cities and territory were quickly regained, and the communists dealt a massive and fatal blow. The Tet Offensive lasted for two months. It was a total military loss for the communist forces. But back in the United States the politicians and the public were shocked and dismayed to see the power and resolve of the communists. Walter Cronkite, a newscaster who was called "the most trusted man in America," departed from his usual objective stance and declared his personal opinion that the war would end in stalemate. His opinion became truth as America lost the political war at nearly the same moment they won the military war in Vietnam.

By the end of 1968 the American people had grown tired of a war they saw as unjust, illegal, and pointless. They opposed the draft, saying it was a way of forcing young men to fight not for their own country, but for obscure political goals in Washington. The Gallup Poll in October 1968 would show that only 37% of people believed it was not a mistake for the U.S. to have entered the war. The number of supporters would decline from there. U.S. troops began to be scaled back, and by 1973 the last of the U.S. troops pulled out as peace accords were signed. But fighting continued until 1975 when the North Vietnamese army captured Saigon, finally uniting the country under communist rule.

😊 😊 😊 EXPLORATION: Timeline

At the end of this unit you will find printable timeline squares. Cut them apart and place them on a wall timeline or in a notebook timeline. The timeline works best when combined with timeline squares from other units so that you can see events from all over the world.

Additional Layer

No formal declaration of war was ever issued by the U.S. Congress for Vietnam. The government called it a "conflict" instead of a war to supposedly avoid the problem of taking a vote for the unpopular war.

Go back and read the Constitution, Article I and then think about why Congress, by law, must be the branch to declare war. Do you think it ought to be necessary for Congress to declare war before missiles are fired or troops are sent? Why or why not?

Famous Folks

William Childs Westmoreland was the U.S. general in charge of the troops in Vietnam.

Additional Layer

The U.S. was supported in the Vietnam War by Australian, South Korean, Filipino, and New Zealand troops.

Additional Layer

Agent Orange was a defoliant chemical that was sprayed across vast swaths of jungle to remove the leaves so the planes and helicopters could see troops and equipment from the air.

It was very effective, but Agent Orange also had terrible consequences for people who inhaled it. Birth defects killed and maimed an estimated 150,000 Vietnamese babies because of the chemical. Adults who were exposed to it have a high risk of cancer, skin diseases, digestive diseases, and respiratory diseases.

For years the U.S. government denied the chemical had any ill health effects to avoid having to pay veterans' medical or retributive costs. To this day, only a small handful of the 39,419 soldiers who have applied for disability based on ill health they suspect was caused by Agent Orange have been granted any financial assistance.

☺ ☺ ☺ EXPLORATION: Map of the Vietnam War

At the end of this unit is a map of the Vietnam War to print. Color the American bases and offensive operations in blue. Color the North Vietnamese offensive operations in red. Color the rivers and seas light blue. Color each country a different color. Notice the location of the Ho Chi Minh trail. The major battles or offensive operations are marked on the map, but by no means is this all of the conflicts. Most conflicts were very small, a single platoon meeting a few Viet Cong somewhere in the trackless jungle or a tiny village being massacred and torched by the Viet Cong. And though it appears as though there were few American offensive actions, most of the American strategy was the bombing of Hanoi and supply lines which lasted throughout the war.

☺ EXPLORATION: War Protestors

The power of opinion in American politics is huge. Vietnam illustrated this very well. In spite of militarily destroying the communists in Vietnam, America was defeated by the home front. Many people just wanted out. People didn't believe in the war anymore. People didn't want to go fight in a war they believed to be unjustified. Some people took an extremist point of view that said all war is always immoral and bad and so are people who engage in it, politicians and soldiers alike.

The American media fueled anti-war sentiment by highlighting American atrocities and ignoring communist ones. They began to give opinion on the nightly newscasts instead of sticking to objective journalism. They also gave a great deal of coverage time to the student protests around the nation. Popular musicians and film stars began openly speaking out against the war. Students on college campuses, egged on by their professors, staged anti-war demonstrations.

Watch this short video about the war protests: https://www.youtube.com/watch?v=vVNUlOUlMeo.

Then watch Walter Cronkite's editorial on the Vietnam War at the end of his nightly news report: https://www.youtube.com/watch?v=Nn4w-ud-TyE. Walter Cronkite was known as "the most trusted man in America" and his unprecedented departure from reporting the facts turned into a self-fulfilling prophecy. Many people started to think that if Cronkite, who was actually in Vietnam and had seen these things first-hand, said we couldn't win, then we couldn't win.

Think about the power of public opinion in a republic where officials are elected. Research more about the Vietnam War protests and some of the major anti-war players of this time, including John Kerry, Jane Fonda, Martin Luther King Jr., Progressive Labor Party, Student Peace Union, and Students for a Democratic Society.

After you've done some research, go interview someone who was alive and old enough to remember 1968 in America. What did they think of the war at the time? What did they think of the protests at the time? Did they serve in Vietnam or closely know someone who did? Did that affect their opinion of the war? Has their opinion changed since then?

Put all the information you've gathered into a report on the protests. Include information from your interview.

☻ EXPLORATION: Nixon's Silent Majority Speech
Watch this 32 minute speech given by President Nixon in 1969 about why America was going to continue fighting in the Vietnam

Additional Layer
The North Vietnamese and the Viet Cong were horrifically brutal. This three year old boy is one of the few survivors of the Viet Cong Dak Son massacre attack on a small village where they systematically murdered 252 civilians.

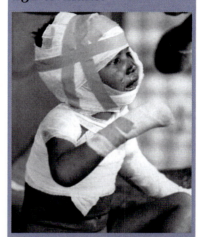

This type of attack was commonplace, and far more Vietnamese civilians died at the hands of their own countrymen than all the military casualties from both sides combined.

Additional Layer
Learn more about John Kerry and Jane Fonda and their activities during the war.

Famous Folks

Not all anti-war protestors were drug culture hippies. Martin Luther King Jr. spoke out against the war as well. You can listen to his speech. https://www.youtube.com/watch?v=b8oBswoUG-U

Additional Layer

The Vietnam War was part of the overall Cold War. The North Vietnamese were communists who brutally enforced their will on the people in the North and then tried to do so in the South, eventually succeeding. They were supported by the Soviets and the Chinese.

At home in America most of the protesters were communists, and they wanted to see an American defeat.

The communists won Vietnam, but they ultimately lost the Cold War. Do you think the communists gave up and went away?

Additional Layer

Another iconic helicopter of the Vietnam era was the Boeing Chinook. Learn more about it. Is it still in use?

War. You may want to print copies of the speech to take notes on and highlight as you listen. http://watergate.info/1969/11/03/nixons-silent-majority-speech.html

Discuss the speech.

- Do you think President Nixon was sincere?
- What were Nixon's arguments for staying in Vietnam for the time being?
- How would abruptly leaving Vietnam affect America according to Nixon?
- What had the United States done up to this point to try to end the war?
- What had been the North Vietnamese response to peace overtures?
- Nixon wanted to end Vietnam and also prevent future Vietnams. How did he say this could be done?
- What do you think of Nixon's plan for future aggression in Asia and around the world, the plan he called Vietnamization?
- Since you know the outcome of the war and have the marvelous gift of hindsight, do you think Nixon did the right thing by pursuing Vietnamization?
- What did Nixon mean by "the silent majority"? People still talk a lot about the "silent majority." Who are they, and why are they silent? Should they be silent? Who are the vocal minority?
- When Nixon says "we passed on the other side of the road," he is alluding to the parable of the Good Samaritan from the Bible. When he does this, he is making a moral statement that America has a responsibility to aid freedom in the world. Do you think this is true? How should America aid freedom?

☺ ☻ EXPLORATION: Tet Offensive

Learn about the events of the Tet offensive and create a newscast of the battle. Be journalistic and refrain from giving your opinion, just the facts. Video yourself. Then you can edit the video to include images of the Tet offensive you find on the internet.

☺ ☻ EXPLORATION: Huey

The Bell UH-1 Iroquois helicopter, nicknamed the Huey, was first used in the Vietnam War. It was meant as a medical evacuation and general utility helicopter. During the war in Vietnam soldiers were spread across the countryside, usually in small patrols. They often came under fire unexpectedly, far from ground support. The courageous helicopter crews would fly right into the hot zones and evacuate wounded soldiers back to the bases. The Huey would also drop soldiers or supplies off at points where enemy activity had been detected or was suspected. The Vietnam War had no front lines, just miles and miles of fields and jungles filled with the enemy.

Make a helicopter out of random supplies from your house, food packaging, paper, toilet paper rolls, or whatever else you have on hand. Craft sticks or straws make good propellers.

☺ ☻ EXPLORATION: Dogs of War

The war in Vietnam was almost completely a guerrilla war, where booby traps or ambushes were set up in the jungle. The American soldiers rarely saw their attackers. It was very nerve-racking and difficult. One of the things the army did to help was to train dogs to sniff out explosives, food caches, and hidden humans. The dogs could warn the soldiers when a booby trap or ambush was on the trail up ahead. Some dogs were used to find the enemy by tracking him. There were over 4,000 dogs sent to Vietnam. It's estimated that they saved over 10,000 lives.

Learn more about the war dogs and write a short account of them and what they did in Vietnam, from the point of view of a dog.

Make a dog puppet from a paper lunch sack. Have the dog puppet "read" the report to an audience.

☺ ☻ ☻ EXPLORATION: American Soldier

At the end of this unit you will find a "Vietnam Diorama Figures" worksheet to print. Color the figures. Then make a jungle background in a shoe box. Add the figures into the diorama.

Take special note of the young lieutenant who is escorting locals out of the fighting zone. American soldiers were often blamed for being brutal and uncaring. When they got home, one of the most common names they were called was "baby killer." There were a few terrible incidents, but far and away American soldiers in every conflict have shown compassion far beyond what was strictly necessary or expected of them.

Famous Folks

Some people think if the Americans had never gone into Vietnam the South Vietnamese would have peacefully chosen communism on their own and all would have been hunky-dory. But experience tells a different story. No nation that adopted communism ever did it peacefully.

North Vietnam went communist without much international interference, but they used a systematic policy of terror to do so. Millions fled south at the communist takeover, and hundreds of thousands were killed, some of them being raped and tortured first.

In South Vietnam, after the war was over and Saigon had fallen, the communists proceeded to march the citizens to "re-education camps" where at least 165,000 prisoners died. Another 200,000 were executed outright and about 50,000 died while performing hard labor.

The fall of Vietnam also led directly to the communist rise in Cambodia where Pol Pot killed an estimated 3 million of his own people out of a population of 8 million.

Additional Layer

In 1955 the South Vietnamese people had a vote on whether to keep the monarchy or become a republic. The vote was rigged by the Americans to favor a republic with 98.2% of the vote. It was this meddling, along with the high non-combatant casualties, that turned opinion against America.

Additional Layer

The My Lai Massacre was a mass killing of between 347 and 504 unarmed civilians in March of 1968 by American soldiers. The incident created a huge storm of outrage when it was found out more than a year later and fueled anti-war sentiment across the globe.

The military tried to hush up the incident, but a helicopter pilot named Warrant Officer Hugh Thompson wouldn't sit back and let it go.

The accounts of the massacre are graphic and disturbing, so look it up with your older kids if you feel they can handle it. Juniors and seniors in high school should probably know about it. Remember, we need to learn history so we do not repeat the mistakes of the past.

We found dozens of images of American soldiers carrying small children and old women out of harm's way, often at the risk of their own lives. American soldiers treated the wounded, fed the hungry, and saved countless lives, while the countrymen of these same people were bent on their suffering and destruction.

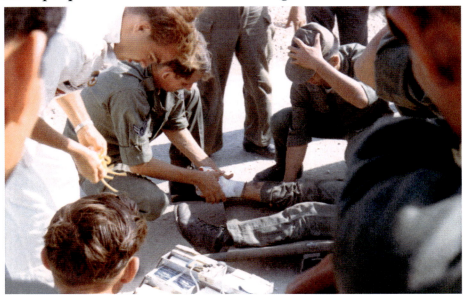

American soldiers are treating a South Vietnamese soldier whose foot was blown off when he stepped on a land mine. No one could figure out how to get the injured man out without setting off the whole mine field. Airman First Class (A1C) William Hart Pittsenbarger said, "No problem, just lower me down on the penetrator, I'll straddle the guy, pick him up, and then you can lift me up." Everyone knew the prop wash (wind coming off the helicopter's props) could blow the whole mine field, including Pittsenbarger, but he did it anyway, saving the young Vietnamese man's life.

American soldiers wrote home, telling their families how desperately in need of clothing and food the people were, and Americans responded with clothing drives. Soldiers helped dress little children and gave mothers warm blankets to wrap their babies in. They volunteered during their off-duty time to help run makeshift schools for little Vietnamese boys and girls. Far and away, most American soldiers are both heroic and compassionate. That's why they do what they do.

☺ ☺ ☺ EXPLORATION: The Fall of Saigon

The Americans had stopped fighting the war in Vietnam in April of 1973. For the next two years, the Americans watched as the South Vietnamese struggled on alone, trying desperately to keep the communists from taking over their country. But on the 30th of April in 1975 the communists took Saigon, and the war was over.

In the last weeks and days Saigon was still full of American soldiers and diplomatic employees who had to be evacuated. Along with them were hundreds of thousands of South Vietnamese who also wanted to flee the coming regime. Operation Baby Lift airlifted about 2,000 war orphans from the city while the planes were being shot at by the enemy. Then Operation Frequent Wind evacuated around 7,000 people by helicopter from the city in the last few days before it fell.

Make a game board with squares along a path. On some of the squares write down events of the fall of Saigon. Roll a die to move along the board and see who can get out of Saigon first.

😊 😊 EXPLORATION: The Boat People

After the U.S. military pulled out and left the defense of Vietnam to the South Vietnamese army it didn't take long for the country to fall. During the final days of the war, and for many months afterward, the North Vietnamese army and the Viet Cong systematically slaughtered their countrymen. Millions were killed. Millions fled. The only place left to go to was the sea.

They boarded fishing boats and merchant vessels and set sail with what water and food they could manage. Thousands upon thousands died at sea of hunger, thirst, and storms. Some made it to Indonesia or were picked up from the sea by other ships, many of them U.S. navy vessels which were searching the oceans for them. Those who were rescued eventually made their way to Australia or to the United States. Many families were broken up and never reunited. A few of the lucky ones found their fathers, brothers, sisters, and children again.

Read accounts of Vietnamese refugees from http://www.migrationheritage.nsw.gov.au/stories/from-there-to-here/from-there-vietnam-to-here-australia/.

This audio interview about an author who wrote a book about the boat people http://www.wnyc.org/story/295657-boat-people-and-vietnam-exodus/.

And this 24 minute documentary from the son of a Vietnamese refugee who fled the war zone and death. http://youtu.be/YNe897ereaY.

These Vietnamese people are being rescued by the USS Blue Ridge after being at sea for 8 days.

Additional Layer

The Khmer Rouge was the communist party of Cambodia. They were an offshoot of the communist party of North Vietnam and allied with the North Vietnamese during the Vietnam War.

In 1975 they overthrew the government of Cambodia and installed Pol Pot as dictator. Between 1975 and 1979 the government instituted social reforms that led to the deaths of 1.5 to 3 million Cambodians, around a quarter of the total population. The killing only ended when Vietnam defeated Cambodia in a war in 1979.

Watch this personal story about how one family escaped the Killing Fields: https://www.ted.com/talks/sophal_ear_escaping_the_khmer_rouge#t-78122

GEOGRAPHY: ATLANTIC STATES

Teaching Tip

If you are working on the Big Map project, which we began in Unit 4-2, add these states to your map.

Teaching Tip

Turn your regional map of these states into a pictorial map that includes tiny pictures of important landmarks. Here are a few to consider.

Pennsylvania: Benjamin Franklin Bridge, Betsy Ross House, Gettysburg Battlefield, Gobbler's Knob, Liberty Bell, Independence Hall, Valley Forge

New York: Statue of Liberty, Central Park, Empire State Building, Times Square, Niagara Falls

Maryland: Chesapeake and Ohio Canal, National Aquarium, Assateague Island, Fort McHenry

Delaware: Fort Delaware, Fenwick Island State Park and Lighthouse, du Pont Estate, Brandywine Zoo

New Jersey: Atlantic City Boardwalk, Jersey Shore, Cape May Lighthouse, Hoboken Waterfront, Thomas Edison National Historical Park, Lucy the Elephant

Pennsylvania, New York, Maryland, Delaware, and New Jersey are the Atlantic states. They are between the New England and the Appalachian states. The climate in these states is temperate. They have hot summers and cold winters with snowfall every year. Along the Atlantic Coast there is a wide belt of coastal plains, fertile farmland, and the site of the largest urban concentration in the United States. As you move inland you run into hills and then mountains, including the Adirondack, Catskill, Allegheny, and Appalachian mountains. The area was historically covered with deciduous forests, but much of the land has been cleared long ago for farms and urban development.

This is the city of Philadelphia in Pennsylvania. This part of the U.S. has lots of big cities with big populations. There is some beautiful countryside too, but no vast tracts of wilderness.

😊 😊 😊 **EXPLORATION: Maps**
At the end of this unit you will find a regional map of the Atlantic states. You can find maps of each of the individual states (Pennsylvania, Maryland, Delaware, New Jersey, and New York) at Layers-of-learning.com in the geography tab of the printables. Label and color the maps you choose with the aid of a student atlas. If you would like to, you can draw in extra features we didn't include like rivers, mountains, national parks, and so on.

http://layers-of-learning.com/layers-of-learning-printables/

😊 😊 😊 **EXPLORATION: States and Capitals Match-up**
Play an Atlantic states matching game. At the end of this unit you

will find printable cards to cut apart. Lay them out upside down on a table. Chose two and see if they match. You have to know the states and capitals to know whether you've gotten answer right. If they do match, you get to keep the set of cards.

☺ ☺ ☺ EXPLORATION: City Skyline State Facts

At the end of this unit there are printable city skyline cards. This area is very urbanized. Print them out, then hand several out to each child. Have them find facts about this region or about individual states or cities in the region. Write the facts on the back of the cards. When they're done, go hide them. Let the kids search for them and then read them aloud to each other.

☺ ☺ ☺ EXPLORATION: Atlantic States Food

Have an Atlantic states feast!

<u>Pennsylvania Cheese Steak Sandwiches</u>
1.5 pounds raw steak, partially frozen
1 large sweet onion
4 bell peppers, any color
4 tablespoons olive oil
salt
pepper
sliced provolone cheese
6 hoagie rolls

1. Slice the steak very thinly. An electric knife or slicer works best. (Some grocers will slice meat for free in their deli.)
2. Slice the onions very thinly. Slice the peppers into strips. Cook the onions and peppers over medium heat in 2 tablespoons of oil until tender. Set aside.
3. In the remaining oil, cook the beef until cooked through, stirring and turning often. Add salt and pepper to taste.
4. Pile beef, onions, peppers, and cheese onto a hoagie roll to serve.

<u>Delaware Dilly Crab Dip with Veggie Dippers</u>
1/2 pound crab meat or imitation crab meat, flaked
1 teaspoon lemon juice
1 tablespoon fresh chopped dill
1/2 teaspoon ground mustard
dash hot sauce, to taste
8 oz. cream cheese, softened

Combine all the ingredients, then spoon into a baking dish. Heat in the oven for 25 minutes at 350 degrees. Serve hot with veggies for dipping.

Additional Layer

Lancaster County in Pennsylvania is famous for its large Amish population.

There are several sects of Amish, all with differing beliefs. Many of them stick to the old ways, avoiding new technology like electricity, automobiles, computers, and so on.

Lancaster County has an interesting history including a border war with Maryland. Learn more.

Fabulous Fact

8.3 million people live in New York City. This is more than the combined populations of Chicago and Los Angeles.

This is Chinatown in New York City.

Famous Folks

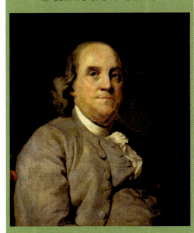

Benjamin Franklin is one of the most famous people from this region. He was born in Boston, Massachusetts, but lived out most of his life in Philadelphia. He was one of America's founders, an ambassador to France, a scientist, a printer and editor, a writer, the U.S. postmaster general, an inventor, a political theorist, and an abolitionist. He may just have been the most accomplished American of all time.

Additional Layer

The Maryland Flag is the only U.S. flag based on Old World heraldry. Learn how it came about.

New Jersey Saltwater Taffy

2 cups sugar
1 cup light corn syrup
1 teaspoon salt
1 1/2 cups water
2 tablespoons butter
1/4 teaspoon food coloring
3/4 teaspoon flavoring extract of your choice

1. Combine sugars, salt, and water in a sauce pan. Cook and stir over medium heat until the sugar all dissolves.
2. Stop stirring and continue to heat until it reaches 260° F.
3. Remove from heat and mix in remaining ingredients. Pour into a buttered jelly roll pan. Let cool until you can handle it. It should still be quite warm.
4. Butter your hands, and stretch and pull the taffy. Fold it, and pull it again. Keep buttering your hands and pulling the taffy until it is no longer sticking to your hands.
5. Divide into fourths. Pull each fourth into a long, thin rope. Cut into pieces with buttered scissors. Wrap individually in waxed paper.

Maryland Senate Bean Soup

Bean soup is served every day in the U.S. senate cafeteria and has been since the early 20th century. One story says that in 1907 Senator Knute Nellson of Minnesota declared a resolution that the bean soup should be served every day and, except for one day during the rationing of World War II when the kitchen ran out of beans, it has been.

2 pounds dried navy beans (or cans of navy beans for a shortcut)
4 quarts hot water
1 1/2 pounds smoked ham hocks (or diced ham for a shortcut)
1 onion, chopped
2 tablespoons butter
salt and pepper to taste

1. Wash the navy beans and run hot water through them until they are slightly whitened. Place beans into pot with hot water. Add ham hocks and simmer approximately three hours in a covered pot, stirring occasionally.
2. Remove ham hocks and set aside to cool. Dice meat and return to soup. Lightly brown the onion in butter. Add to soup.
3. Before serving, bring to a boil and season with salt and pepper. Serves 8.

New York Cheesecake

5 graham crackers, crushed

2 tablespoons butter, melted
4 (8 ounce) packages cream cheese
1 1/2 cups white sugar
3/4 cup milk
 4 eggs
1 cup sour cream
1 tablespoon vanilla extract
1/4 cup all-purpose flour

1. Mix graham cracker crumbs with melted butter. Press into the bottom of a springform pan.
2. Mix remaining ingredients in a large bowl with an electric mixer. Pour onto the graham cracker crust.
3. Bake at 350° F for 1 hour. Turn off the oven and let the cake sit and cool inside the oven for 2 hours. Chill in refrigerator.
4. Serve with blueberry pie filling poured over the top.

☺ ☻ EXPLORATION: Atlantic City

Make a paper model of Atlantic City, New Jersey. Include the beach and boardwalk on a piece of flat poster board. Make hotels and restaurants and shops and beach huts out of card stock. Color the buildings brightly. Add triangle-shaped paper stands to the back.

☺ ☻ ☻ EXPLORATION: Erie Canal

The Erie Canal was the first transport system between the eastern seaboard and the Great Lakes region. It runs east to west right through New York. The Erie Canal is still used today, mostly for

Additional Layer

There is a local legend in the Pine Barrens region of southern New Jersey about a creature that lives there. It is known as the Jersey Devil. Go read the tale.

Fabulous Fact

The game, Monopoly, is based on the geography of Atlantic City. Park Place and Boardwalk, the Reading Railroad and Illinois Avenue are all in Atlantic City.

On the Web

Watch this time lapse video about the locks of the Erie Canal and see them fill up to raise the water level and the watercraft inside too. It's called "Erie Canal Locks Time Lapse HD Video" by Aaron Pufal.

https://youtu.be/S7_Hr3iCPls

Library List

This book by Peter Spier uses the lyrics from "Low Bridge, Everybody Down."

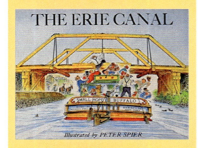

THE ERIE CANAL

Illustrated by PETER SPIER

This is a book by Cheryl Harness that tells the story of the construction of the canal.

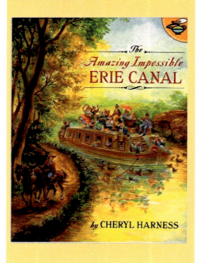

The Amazing Impossible ERIE CANAL

by CHERYL HARNESS

On The Web

Take a quick walking tour of Philadelphia on this YouTube video, "Tour Philadelphia in 4 Minutes!" by Lissa Coffey. You'll see landmarks like the Liberty Bell and also get a glimpse at a normal day in Philadelphia.

https://youtu.be/4SfX-ae5CbzU

recreation, but there is still some shipping along the route.

Watch this ten minute history about the canal "200 years on the Erie Canal": https://www.youtube.com/watch?v=iLfGSXuHu5g

Then complete the printable Erie Canal map from the end of this unit. Print the map onto card stock. Trace over the route of the Erie Canal. Find it on a wall map or in an atlas as well. Cut a slit along each of the dotted lines. Make a strip of card stock that can fit inside the slits. Draw the lock doors and water levels in frames on your long strip so that as you pull the paper through the slots, the locks fill up.

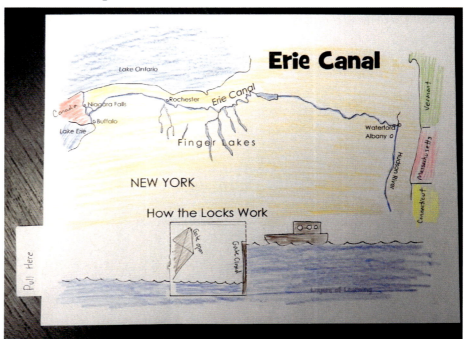

☺ ☻ **EXPLORATION: Delaware Beaches**

In the summertime everyone heads for the beautiful Delaware beaches along the southern coast in the state. There are little towns filled with restaurants, shopping, golf courses, and boardwalks, as well as the sun and the sand.

Make a beach notebook page with paper cut out sand pails, star fish, sea shells, sand castles, beach balls, and so on. Leave each item glued only on one edge so it creates a flap. Behind each flap write down a fact about Delaware that you have researched in a book or online.

☺ ☻ EXPLORATION: Pennsylvania Zoo

The Philadelphia Zoo was the first in the United States. Besides functioning as entertainment for guests, the zoo educates the public about animals and conservation, studies species, preserves endangered species, and reintroduces them to the wild.

Explore the Philadelphia Zoo website a bit, learning about animals and some of the zoo's features. http://www.philadelphiazoo.org/

Then make a zoo of your own. You will need toy zoo animals and a variety of cardboard boxes, along with paper, scissors, and glue. Each cardboard box will be an enclosure for a different animal. Start by spray painting the outside of each box in bright colors. Fill the cardboard box with paper plants, water, and soil for the animal to live in. Arrange the enclosures the way you like them and play with your zoo animals.

Fabulous Fact

Every New Year's Day the city of Philadelphia has a Mummer's Parade. People dress in elaborate costumes and march through the streets, playing in bands and dancing. The tradition dates back to the beginning of the city when Swedish immigrants would dress in costume around Christmas time and demand ale and food from their neighbors.

This is an especially elaborate costume from the 2011 parade.

☺ ☻ EXPLORATION: Maryland's Chesapeake Bay

The Chesapeake Bay is a huge estuary that cuts right up through the middle of Maryland. It is the outlet for more than 150 major rivers and streams, including the Susquehanna and the Potomac rivers. Watch "Chesapeake Bay By Air" from

Additional Layer

Pennsylvania is the home of the Hershey chocolate company. Make this Hershey's cake:

1 cup butter
1 1/4 cups sugar
4 eggs
6 Hershey bars
2 1/2 cups flour
1/4 tsp. baking soda
dash salt
1 cup buttermilk
1/2 cup Hershey syrup
2 tsp. vanilla

Bake 1 hour at 350° F.

YouTube: https://youtu.be/FpJz1wsF6Z8.

People dredge for oysters from the bay using sailing boats called skipjacks. Powered boats are restricted by law from the oyster fisheries, so the sailing boats are still used today. Paint a picture of a skipjack on the Chesapeake Bay.

☺ ☺ ☺ EXPLORATION: Baltimore Oriole

The Baltimore Oriole is the state bird of Maryland. The orange and black colors are in the Calvert family coat of arms, which appears on the state flag.

Find a tutorial on how to draw a bird. After you've drawn your bird, color it to look like a Baltimore Oriole. Write a paragraph about how the bird represents Maryland.

☺ ☺ EXPLORATION: People of the Atlantic States

The Mid-Atlantic region is one of the most diverse areas in the United States. People from all over the world immigrate to New York, New Jersey, and Pennsylvania, in particular. Jews, Hispanics, Blacks, Middle Easterners, Europeans, Chinese, Vietnamese, and many more people from various nationalities and races have found homes in these American states.

Make finger puppet people with all different colors of skin and hair to show what the people of these states look like. There is a basic outline of puppet shapes to print at the end of this unit.

Use heavy paper like card stock. Dress your people with more card stock or fabric, wiggly eyes, crayons, and permanent markers. Cut out the holes at the bottom and then insert your fingers through to be the legs.

Look up the numbers of population demographics and make a chart or graph showing the races by percent.

☺ ☻ ☻ EXPLORATION: Baseball Review

Have each child pick a team from these states (more than one can be on a single team if you like). Then play a fact baseball game.

Here are the teams you can choose from:

- New York Yankees
- New York Mets
- Baltimore Orioles
- Philadelphia Phillies

Look up where the cities these teams are from are located on a map.

Set up a "baseball diamond" in your living room or in the backyard. Have the kids answer review questions about the states in this unit or about any of the states you have covered so far this year. For every correct question they get to move forward a base. If they miss a question they get a "strike" and have to stay where they are. If they get three strikes, they're out! First one to home plate wins.

At the end of this unit we provide a sheet of review questions for the pitcher (Mom or Dad) to ask, but add as many of your own as you like. There are also "strike" cards to hand to the kids so you can keep track of strikes (missed questions). There are team logos to tape on to their shirts. If there is more than one kid on a team, allow them to consult and answer the questions together.

☻ ☻ EXPLORATION: America's Freedom

One of the things that makes America America is freedom. That freedom was fostered in colonial days in these middle states, between the sectionalism of New England, with its strict Puritan and English roots, and the South, with its harshly segregated plantation society. That history is essential to where these states are today. They are still the most diverse and tolerant of just about anywhere in America.

Make a poster showing some of the freedoms that were fostered in these states. Remember economic, personal, religious, speech, and others. Illustrate the poster.

Writer's Workshop

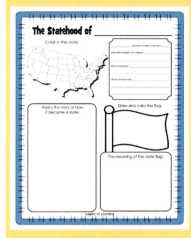

Make a statehood notebooking page about one or more of the states from this region. Find out the story of how it became a state and learn about the state's flag and what it means. You'll find a printable statehood notebooking page in the geography printables on Layers-of-Learning.com.

http://layers-of-learning.com/layers-of-learning-printables/

Writer's Workshop

Make your own "fun facts" miniature booklet about one of these states. Cut sheets of paper into quarter-sized sheets. Look up interesting facts and record one per page of your booklet. Illustrate the pages. You can use a simple staple binding or have it bound at a local copy center.

SCIENCE: FOOD CHAINS

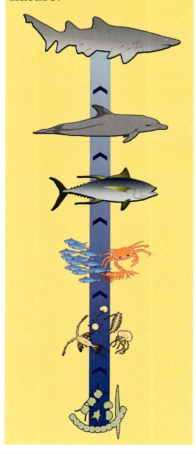

Animals and plants live in an interactive world in nature. Plants live off of the sun and nutrients from the soil, which are provided by the decaying of other once-living organisms. Animals live off of plants and each other. The water, air, and soil are all affected by the living and mineral world. And the living world is affected by the water, air, and mineral world. There is an incredibly complex web of interactions between living and non-living elements in a particular environment. If something affects one element of that environment, it has some sort of repercussions on the whole. If a forest is burned, for example, the entire animal and plant life of the area is radically affected. If a stream is polluted, the entire ecology of the region is affected. If one predator moves into a swamp, the life of the swamp is altered in some way. Everything is connected.

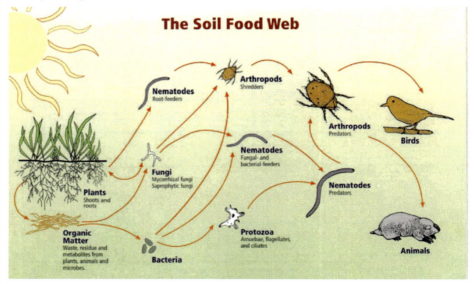

Some of the changes in an environment, even radical ones, are normal, natural, and usually even desirable. A volcanic explosion is a radical change that no one could deny is incredibly destructive. But the volcano also clears away old forests and makes way for new life. A volcano creates new land and new soil and changes the course of streams. It is a beginning as well as an end. Other environmental changes are nothing but destructive, with no benefits. The polluting of soil, water, or air by humans would fit in this category.

Not everything humans do to the environment is bad though. Logging with an eye to the future forest actually makes a forest healthier. Hunting with management makes for healthier deer and elk populations and reduces problems with predators living too near to humans. And damming a river for floodwater management, irrigation, and power production, while it radically alters the environment, also creates new clean habitats for animals and plants and clean energy for people to use.

The study of plants and animals and how they interact together with human activities is the study of ecology.

😊 😊 EXPLORATION: Timeline of Ecology

Ecology is a new science. Studying the environment as a series of connected events, instead of studying each animal or plant one by one, only began about one hundred and fifty years ago. Ecology is also the most complex of all sciences. It incorporates knowledge about minerals, animals, animal biology, plants and plant systems, water, air, soil, and insects, and tosses them together with chemistry and physiology to study entire systems of living and non-living things. As such, ecology is still only in its baby stages as a science. We really understand very little about how adding or subtracting one element from a system will affect that system. As a result, humans have made a lot of mistakes in the past regarding the natural environment, even when their intentions were good.

It's important to have a proper perspective of ecology as a science and to understand its purpose and limitations. That's why it is important to understand the history of ecology. At the end of this unit you will find a history of ecology printable to put together and color. The timeline pieces are out of order. So kids will have to cut them apart and glue them in order on several pieces of paper. The papers they glue them to should have heavy lines drawn down the center with hash marks for decades.

Below we included the timeline in order and with notes so you can talk about the new terms the kids will come across in the timeline. Feel free to insert your own input as well.

- Late 1700s Antoine Lavoisier, a chemist, discovered oxygen and carbon and their importance to living things.
- 1852 Robert Angus Smith connected acid rain to air pollution
- 1869 Ernst Haeckel coins the term "ecology." *Ecology is the study of how elements in an environment react and interact with one another. It includes plants, animals, air, water, and earth, as well as humans, all in an ecosystem.*
- 1875 Eduard Seuss defined the biosphere. *Biosphere is all the living things on earth. It is the living layer of earth.*
- 1879 Symbiosis was first described. *Symbiosis is when two living organisms live together for their mutual benefit, like the plover that cleans the crocodiles' teeth. The plover gets*

On the Web

"Introduction to Ecology" by Teachers Pet is a great introduction to this unit for middle grades and up: https://www.youtube.com/watch?v=GlnFyl-wdYH4

Famous Folks

Ernst Haeckel was a German biologist who traveled the world, going to exotic locations to discover new species.

He made thousands of detailed drawings that are still popular as art.

Teaching Tip

The timeline of ecology mentions several ecological concepts that are not covered in this unit. Rest assured, they are covered in later units in this curriculum.

On the Web

With your high school students, begin this unit by watching "Ecology Introduction" from Khan Academy: https://www.youtube.com/watch?v=OfV3VNgjpvw

Fabulous Fact

Ecologists have four aims:

1. Understand how and why life does what it does.
2. Study energy transfer through living systems.
3. Trace successional development of environments.
4. Study the abundance and distribution of life.

Ecology is the study of how living things interact.

An ecologist studying this coral reef would want to know how the animals, plants, water, and rocks affect each other.

food and the crocodile gets a clean mouth.

- Late 1800s Animal camouflage studied and described. *Camouflage means an animal is hard to see because its hide, skin, or markings match or blend with the natural background it lives in. Camouflage helps a predator sneak up on prey and it helps prey to hide from predators.*
- 1900 Henry Chandler Cowles studied ecological succession. *Ecological succession happens after a fire, volcano, mudslide, or other event that completely clears a natural environment. First, fireweed and grasses come back, then bushes, then small, fast-growing trees. Finally, slower growing, but taller trees grow so big that they shade the ground, and the smaller fast- growing trees, grasses, bushes and weeds die out.*
- 1915 Ecological Society of America founded. *The ESA is a professional organization of ecological scientists. It publishes a peer reviewed journal for ecological studies to be published in. They also work to educate the public and influence public policy.*
- 1927 Charles Elton made the concept of food chains and webs part of ecology. *Food chains and food webs describe how animals and plants are connected when they eat each other.*
- 1933 Aldo Leopold wrote Game Management, beginning the discipline of wildlife management. *Wildlife management attempts to balance the needs of animal populations with human usage, like hunting and fishing and controlling predator populations.*
- 1935 The Dust Bowl crisis re-focused ecology on practical land usage practices. *The Dust Bowl made people realize that the soil is held together by plant roots. If there are no plants, then the soil can blow or wash away. Topsoil is formed slowly over long periods of time and, once gone, it cannot be replaced. So people realized they had to take care of the whole land with a view to the future, not just the next harvest.*
- 1935 Arthur Tinsley defined ecosystem. *An ecosystem is a particular environment when animals, plants, and the earth interact. The largest ecosystem is the entire earth; the smallest ecosystems can be a square foot of soil or smaller. An ecosystem can be whatever space a person defines.*
- 1940s Ruth Patrick studied interdependence of organisms, particularly freshwater ecosystems. She developed methods to measure the health of a stream.
- 1950s People first became aware of the harmful effects of pollution on ecological systems and on people. *Often the Industrial Revolution is criticized as an ecologically irresponsible disaster, but people honestly didn't know what the results of*

pollution would be. After all, smokestacks had never belched out smoke and sewage had never been dumped in such volume into streams. They really did think it would all just go away. Experience is a great teacher.

- 1951 Nature Conservancy was founded. *The Nature Conservancy is a non-profit organization whose mission is to preserve in pristine condition as many wild lands as they can. They do allow mining, oil drilling, hunting, and logging on lands they preserve when it is done responsibly.*

- 1953 Eugene and Howard Odum wrote the first ecology textbook and ecology became a university course.

- 1970s James Lovelock's idea of Gaia was formulated; the whole earth is one living entity and will ensure its own survival even if humans destroy themselves. *Gaia is a sort of mystical mother-earth movement, but it's important because the environmental movement has been hugely influenced by it. Gaia has changed efforts to preserve and restore the natural world into a "religious" movement, though that word is not used to describe environmentalism by its acolytes.*

- 1972 Acid rain effects on lakes was discovered and studied by Harold Harvey. *Acid rain is rain that includes dissolved carbon dioxide from factory smokestacks. It kills trees, dissolves rock, and kills fish in ponds. Entire valleys in industrialized areas were dead in the 1970s, but today in the United States they have all recovered and are growing green again. It is still a problem in some nations like Russia and China.*

- 1978 Conservation biology established as a discipline that focuses on environmental management

- 1980s Scientists discovered a hole in the ozone over Antarctica. *The ozone layer hole was discovered in the 1980s, but no one knows how long it has actually been there. Maybe its natural and maybe it really is caused by humans. Either way, it alarmed people and has influenced laws and regulations in the United States and other developed nations.*

- 1980s Water pollution seriously reduced due to new sewage treatment practices. *In spite of ever higher levels of consumption and production, the earth is cleaner than it has been in several hundred years. Formerly polluted lakes and rivers can recover. Technology and the law caught up.*

- 1980s Air pollution reduced in cities as unleaded gas and catalytic converters are used in autos. *Most of the air pollution in large cities today comes from cars, not factory smokestacks.*

☺ ☻ EXPLORATION: Food Chain
A food chain tells us how animals are related to each other based

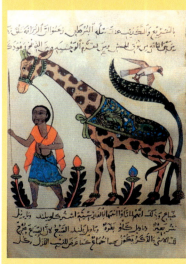
on what they eat. A mouse eats the seeds from the grass. The owl eats the mouse. The grass, the mouse, and the owl are all part of a food chain.

Here's another food chain. Who is eating who in this chain?

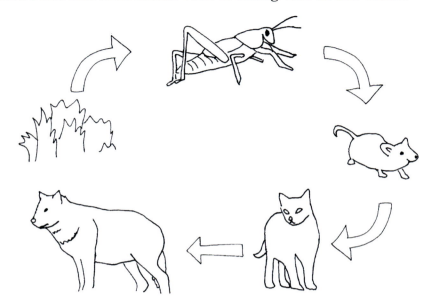

At the end of this unit you will find this food chain in a printable to color.

☺ ☺ EXPLORATION: Food Chains Game

Who eats who? At the end of this unit you will find printable animal game cards. Print the cards on card stock, and cut the cards apart. You can color them if you'd like.

Place all the cards in a stack upside down. Draw a card and turn it face up. Players take turns drawing one card at a time and placing the card to the right of an animal that eats it or to the left of an animal that gets eaten by it. If you can't place a card on an already forming chain, start a new chain. Your goal is to get all of the animals in one of the chains.

☺ ☺ EXPLORATION: Complete-A-Chain

At the end of this unit you will find a worksheet showing several food chains that must be completed. Fill in animals and plants that fit the chain. Everyone who does the worksheet will probably get different answers. For example, many animals eat mice and people eat many things, so answers can be different. If you're not sure what an animal eats, then do a little research.

☺ ☺ ☺ EXPLORATION: Producers and Consumers

Some living things are producers and some are consumers. Producers make food in their bodies using either sunlight or chemical energy. Plants are producers.

Consumers have to eat something else to get energy. Birds, worms, bats, cows, lions, and people are all consumers.

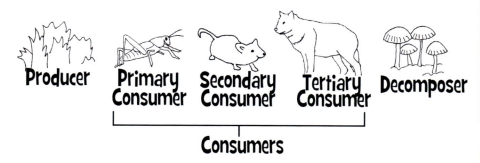

Consumers can be put into categories. Primary level consumers eat plants. A cow is a primary consumer. Secondary level consumers eat animals that eat plants. Tertiary level consumers eat animals that eat animals.

Some animals can be primary, secondary, or tertiary level consumers depending on what's for dinner. For example, people eat plants, cows (which eat plants), as well as seafood (a lot of which is carnivorous). So people are primary, secondary, and tertiary consumers.

A wolf might be a secondary or tertiary consumer. It might eat a deer that grazed on grass or it might eat a mouse that ate a grasshopper that ate a leaf.

Besides this, there are living things that eat nothing but dead material, like dead leaves or dead rotting animals. These are decomposers and scavengers. Mushrooms are decomposers. A vulture is a scavenger. They have an important role in the food chain too.

Use the food chains game cards from the "Food Chains Game" exploration to sort your food chain animals into:

- Producers
- Consumers (primary, secondary, or tertiary)
- Decomposers and scavengers

😊 😊 EXPLORATION: Food Web

Food chains are useful to see how food moves in an environment, but the truth is more complex. There isn't just one animal that wants to eat the mouse. So real interactions in a real environment turn into a web instead of a straight chain. Use the food web worksheet from the end of this unit to connect the animals in a web. Draw arrows pointing in the direction the food moves.

On the Web

"Understanding Ecosystems for Kids: Producers, Consumers, Decomposers" from Free School will help your kids understand the roles of producers, consumers, and decomposers in the environment: https://www.youtube.com/watch?v=bJEToQ49Yjc

Additional Layer

Even though a food web is much more complex than a food chain, it is still extremely simplified.

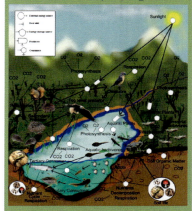

Biologists use scientific models to explain these complex systems.

Additional Layer

Some animals are more than keystone species, they are called engineers. They dramatically change their environment and their activities make life better for many other species of animals.

Prairie dogs are the engineers of the Great Plains, providing burrows and homes for ground nesting birds and other rodents, keeping grass short and growing fast, and helping to channel rainwater run-off to prevent flooding.

Photo by Jeff Kubina, CC license

On the Web

High schoolers can watch "Energy Flow in Ecosystems" from Bozeman Science to learn about trophic levels: https://www. youtube.com/watch?v=l-nAKICtJIA4.

Have your older students start with one wild animal that lives in your region. Research what your animal eats and what eats it. Make a food web centered on your creature.

😊 😊 EXPLORATION: Keystone Species

A keystone species is a species that has a strong effect on its environment, much stronger than the numbers of its population would suggest. If a keystone species is removed from its environment there will be huge repercussions on the whole environment.

A keystone species is usually a low level predator that keeps a population of prey in check. If the predator dies out or leaves the area, the prey will overproduce and destroy the plant population, dramatically changing the environment. It doesn't usually take very many of a keystone species to do the job, and that can make them especially vulnerable. If only a few are killed off or driven out, then the whole environment can collapse.

In 1966 Dr. Robert Paine from the University of Washington described how the starfish in the tidal pools of the coast were a keystone species. The starfish ate the mussels and sea urchins, which have no other predators. In places where the starfish were eliminated the mussel population grew unchecked and out-competed other species. The sea urchins also grew out of control and killed off coral reefs, which they feed on.

Ochre Sea Stars from the Pacific Coast of British Columbia. Photo by D. Gordon E. Robertson, CC license.

Research a keystone species and describe their importance to their environment. Write a report explaining what you found.

😊 😊 EXPEDITION: Trophic Levels

Animals and plants occupy a trophic level that corresponds with where they are on the food chain. Plants are producers, so they are on trophic level one. Squirrels eat seeds from plants and they are primary consumers, so they are on trophic level 2. Cats eat squirrels so they are on trophic level 3. A coyote eats a cat so it is on trophic level 4. The mountain lion that eats the coyote is on trophic level 5. The mountain lion is an apex predator. Nothing eats the mountain lion.

But what does happen to the mountain lion when it dies? Carrion feeders like crows, vultures, and coyotes will eat it. Bacteria will eat it. Flies will eat it. And eventually it will decompose entirely. So decomposers and carrion feeders are in a class of their own and do an important job in nature. They are nature's recyclers.

Observe animals in your backyard, in a nearby park, or in a national forest. Choose one of the animals to do an in-depth study on. What does your animal eat? What hunts it? Observe your animal several times over a couple of weeks. Take good notes on how it interacts with its environment. You may need to do some research in the library or online to find out more. What trophic level does your animal exist on? Is it on more than one trophic level depending on what it is eating?

☺ ☺ ☺ EXPLORATION: Ecological Pyramid

As energy is eaten by an animal on a higher trophic level, most of the energy is used up each time. After 3 or 4 and sometimes 5 links of the food chain, then the energy is gone. There is no such thing as the 6th trophic level. The way this energy is used up and how the populations of the organisms on the trophic levels decrease as you move up the food chain is called the Ecological Pyramid.

There are huge populations of plants. Large populations of primary consumers like deer, rabbits, and mice. Big populations of secondary consumers like coyotes. And small populations of tertiary consumers like mountain lions.

When a grasshopper eats plants, about 10% of the energy eaten goes toward making new individuals for the grasshopper population or growing the size of the grasshopper who did the eating. The rest of the energy, the remaining 90%, goes toward the metabolism of the grasshopper, just keeping it alive. That's why it takes so many plants to support populations of animals on higher trophic levels. At each trophic level the same story happens. 10% of the energy goes toward building the population and the rest just keeps the eater alive.

That's why rabbits produce so rapidly. Their large populations are necessary to support consumers who are higher up the ecological pyramid.

Additional Layer

You will come across the term "biodiversity" in your reading. It just means the variety of life. If you live in a very biodiverse place, then there are lots of different species of plants and animals. If you live in a place with low diversity there may only be a hundred or so different species. A jungle has a much higher biodiversity than a desert.

This is a sample of fungi species collected in a mixed forest in Saskatchewan, Canada. Photo by Sasata, CC by SA 3.0, Wikimedia

The earth as a whole is incredibly biodiverse. Scientists estimate there are 10 to 14 million different species, only about a million of which have been described.

Generally, greater biodiversity is seen as a good thing. Do some research to find out why.

Fabulous Fact

Only about 10% of the energy produced is transfered on to the next trophic level. This is why there is an upper limit of five trophic levels.

The pyramid represented at the right is an energy pyramid. It shows the amount of energy in each level. You can also have pyramids that show biomass (mass of living tissue) at each level or pyramids that show numbers of individuals. A numbers pyramid may be inverted, but a energy pyramid never is and a biomass pyramid only rarely is.

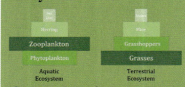

These are numbers pyramids. The one on the left shows fewer phytoplankton individuals than zooplankton in the sea. Image by Swiggity.Swag. YOLO.Bro, CC by SA 4.0.

Additional Layer

Not all introduced species become invasive. What factors create a problem?

On the Web

Watch "The threat of invasive species" from Ted-Ed to learn about invasive species. https://youtu.be/spTWwqVP_2s

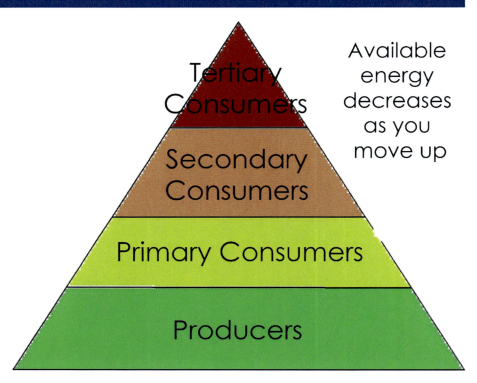

Tertiary Consumers

Secondary Consumers

Primary Consumers

Producers

Available energy decreases as you move up

At the end of this unit is a printable ecological pyramid worksheet. Cut out the tags and glue them to the correct places next to the pyramid. Answers are above on the pyramid. Draw pictures of animals and plants that would fit on each level within the pyramid tiers.

☺ EXPLORATION: Species Introduction

When a new species is introduced to an environment it nearly always disrupts the food chain in wildly unpredictable ways. Sometimes species are introduced accidentally, like the brown tree snake that hitched rides on the landing gear of aircraft and invaded the island of Guam. Sometimes species are introduced on purpose, like the many millions of rainbow trout that have been added to streams across the United States for fishermen to catch.

Find out what happened in Guam with the brown tree snake and find out what effect non-native rainbow trout have on freshwater lakes and streams.

Then learn about this bad boy, the Tiger Muskee, one of the most ferocious creatures ever crafted by man. It made tiny Shepherd Lake in North Idaho uninhabitable both by other species of fish and by people.

Write a research paper about introduced species and the problems they can cause. Can you find an example of when introducing a new species was a good thing?

☺ ☻ ☻ EXPLORATION: Species Extinction

Extinction means the end of a species, that all the individuals have died out, and there will be no more. As we have learned in this unit, every species plays a role in its environment. When one species goes extinct, it affects all the others around it. Scientists estimate that 5 billion different species have lived on the earth in its history. 99% of those species have become extinct. Extinction is a normal and natural process and there are hundreds of complex reasons why a species might go extinct. A tiny portion of those reasons are caused by humans. There isn't much that can (or should) be done about natural extinctions, but human-caused extinction should always be of concern. There are five human-caused reasons that species go extinct:

- Habitat Loss - humans destroy the area where the animal or plant lives
- Introduced Species - humans move a species to a new area where it out-competes the native animals or plants
- Pollution - the environment is damaged by humans, making it unfit for life
- Population growth - humans use more and more land for cities and farms, leaving less for animals
- Overconsumption - Humans use the species until there are no more left

Look up information on specific extinct or endangered animals and plants and determine the cause of their extinction. Make a poster that explains the causes of extinction and includes pictures and information on the species you researched.

☻ EXPLORATION: Current Events

In Lake Pend Oreille (Pond Or-Ay), North Idaho, watermilfoil weeds are a big problem. Milfoil is an invasive aquatic plant. It grows rapidly and chokes up waterways, prevents sunlight from reaching the bottom of lakes and rivers, and makes the water unusable for recreation. Milfoil was introduced from Europe. Since it isn't native, local species can't keep it under control naturally. So people want to get rid of it. There are lots of suggestions. We could spread chemical herbicides. We could pick it by hand. We could use underwater mowing machines to keep it down. Or we could introduce another species, the water weevil, to eat the plants. At Lake Pend Oreille the problem still hasn't been solved and from time to time a debate over it breaks out.

Find out what environmental debates over species populations are happening in your area. Search the news and learn about all sides of the argument. What do you think is the right solution?

Memorization Station

Endangered animals are sorted into categories based on how in danger they are. Learn these categories. Here they are from most threatened to least:

Extinct (EX)
Extinct in the Wild (EW)
Critically Endangered (CR)
Endangered (EN)
Vulnerable (VU)
Near Threatened (NT)
Conservation Dependent (CD)
Least Concern (LC)

Expedition

Zoos are heavily involved in researching and preserving endangered species. Visit a zoo near you and make a point of learning about the endangered species the zoo is involved with.

Fabulous Fact

Almost all of the information you will find in books and online is about animals that have gone extinct or are endangered because of humans. This will make it appear that humans are the reason that all species go extinct, but this is far from the truth.

THE ARTS: PHOTOGRAPHY

Memorization Station

Learn these photography terms.

Composition: the way things are arranged in your photograph

Resolution: the quality of your photo, based on how many pixels per inch

Exposure: the amount of light coming into the camera (based on a combination of aperture and shutter speed)

Aperture: lens opening

Shutter Speed: How long the camera's shutter is open

Depth of Field: How much of the image is in focus

We're going to learn a little bit about the history of photography, some famous photographers, and a bit about how cameras work in this unit. Mostly, we're going to take lots of photos. One of the best ways to become a photography artist is to start taking pictures. As you take pictures, try to think like an artist. Look for interesting colors, textures, lines, shapes, and patterns. Try to be aware of creating unity and balance in your photos. We'll learn a few tricks and tips from photographers that will help you take pictures like an artist.

Fabulous Fact

These days people take more pictures in one year than were taken in the entire century of the 1800s. Trillions of photos are taken each year now, and most people carry a camera with them in their phone. Many of those photos are then shared on social media accounts. Photography is no longer just for the wealthy or artistic. It's for everyone.

☺ ☺ ☺ EXPLORATION: Photography, A History

The idea of a camera stemmed from the camera obscura, which was a way to capture an image using light in the 1500s, much like a simple projector. The very first commercial camera was invented in 1839 by Louis Daguerre. It took several minutes for a picture, called a daguerreotype, to be produced. Along the way, many inventions transformed early cameras to make them better and better. George Eastman revolutionized cameras and put them into the hands of regular, everyday people when he began the Kodak company and began selling affordable cameras. Since that time cameras have gotten much faster and much more detailed.

Watch the video called "History of Photography" by Gavin Seim on YouTube. Create your own illustrated timeline with small pictures that represent each event. https://youtu.be/ZijSBjOVCBo

☺ ☺ ☺ EXPLORATION: Label A Camera

Use the "Label A Camera" printable to learn the parts of a camera and see where the light is being reflected inside of the camera. If you have access to one, look at a real camera and try to identify its external parts. If you have the us-

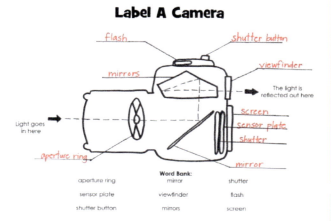

er's manual for your camera, either printed or online, it will be able to tell you the names of all of the parts of your specific camera model. Most manuals also tell you what each part does and give instructions for your camera's settings.

☺ ☺ EXPLORATION: Pinhole Camera

You can make your own pinhole camera to see how the early camera obscura worked. You'll need a shoe box that's painted black, a 3" square piece of waxed paper, tape, an Xacto knife, and a needle. Start by making a pinhole with the needle in one side of the shoe box. On the opposite side, directly across from the pinhole, cut out a 2 inch square from the shoe box. Tape the waxed paper directly over the hole.

Stand about 5 feet from a lamp and cover your head and the camera with a blanket to make sure it's really dark. Point the pinhole at the lamp, and keep the waxed paper facing you. Hold the box really steady until you begin to see the image of a lamp appear. It will be upside down and backwards.

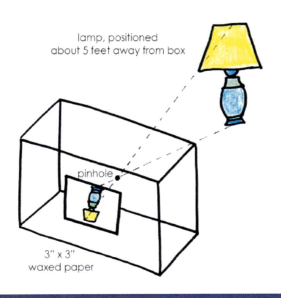

The pinhole is like a camera lens. It lets in light. The waxed paper is like film. It records the image on its surface when light hits it.

Famous Folks

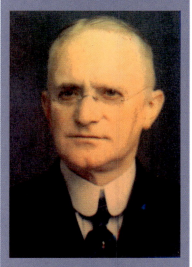

George Eastman founded the Eastman Kodak Company. He patented roll film, designed and produced cameras, and made photography available to many people through his inexpensive versions of cameras. He was a successful businessman and a generous philanthropist who donated over $100 million. He also helped set up schools, build up college campuses, and create heath clinics.

Fabulous Fact

The word "photography" originates from Greek and means drawing with light.

Famous Folks

Although he didn't have any formal college degree, Edwin Land was an inventor and a scientist. He worked on everything from night vision goggles to color film. In 1943, his three-year-old daughter wanted to see the picture he took of her right away. She inspired him to invent the Polaroid camera, which developed pictures almost instantly. He was very progressive, hiring women and minorities for research and management positions within his company. He also served as an advisor to U.S. President Dwight D. Eisenhower. He helped with many military applications of photography and optics, including working on spy planes and technology that could detect enemy camouflage.

☺ ☺ EXPLORATION: Pixelated Picture

A pixel is just a dot. Digital photos are made up of colorful pixels, or tiny dots of color, that when placed side by side, make the picture. The more pixels there are in each square inch, the higher the quality of the photo. If you keep zooming in further and further, eventually you will see the pixels on a photograph.

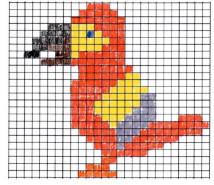

Use the "Pixelated Picture" printable to make your own picture using colorful dots.

☺ ☺ ☺ EXPLORATION: Just The Right Light

The word photo means light. Photographs use light to capture images. In fact, lighting is one of the most important elements of photography. Great lighting often makes for a great photograph.

A lot of people think that taking pictures is best done with lots of sunlight. Sunlight is actually really harsh in photographs though, and it also creates unattractive shadows and glares.

In the mornings and late afternoons or evenings the sunlight is diffused. Because the sun is lower on the horizon, the light is spread out more and less direct. This soft sunlight creates lighting that is easier to photograph. Photographers call the hour after the sun rises and the hour before the sun sets a "golden hour."

It can also be nice to take pictures on overcast days, when the sun is being blocked by clouds. If it's really sunny, you might need to find a spot in the shade. Just make sure you aren't halfway in the sun and halfway in the shade; the dappled light doesn't look good, especially if your subject is being half shaded. Take some photographs in the morning, afternoon, and evening. Compare the lighting. Can you spot the softness of a golden hour?

☺ ☺ ☺ EXPLORATION: Ansel Adams

Ansel Adams is one of the most famous photographers to ever live. He really loved the outdoors and spent a lot of time hiking and taking photographs in the American West. He enjoyed nature and loved to capture its beauty. He did some color photography, but preferred to work in black and white. You can learn all about him, both his life and his work, on anseladams.com.

Make a Shutterflap book about Ansel Adams. Use the printable from the end of this unit and cut along the solid lines. Go online and research information about him, then lift the flaps and write down what you learned from your research under each topic. Find at least 10 photographs he took that include nature or the outdoors to see what his photographs looked like. Tell someone about what you learned about his life and his photography.

☺ ☺ EXPLORATION: Subject and Frame

Which would you rather have - a hundred photos that aren't any good or one really amazing shot?

These days we take lots and lots of photos, especially since digital photography is so easy and inexpensive. But in our frenzy to take lots of pictures, often we still fail to get a really great shot. There's a lot that goes into a great photo, but it all starts with your subject and scene. If you were painting a picture you would spend a bit of time thinking about your subject - the part you want to feature, also called the focal point. Then you would think about the best way to show it off in your overall scene, what else to include that will make your focal point look fantastic. You can do the same thing with a photograph.

Go outside with a camera. Decide on a subject for your photo. It could be your friend who is hanging out with you, an apple on a tree, your dog, an icicle on your roof, or an ant crawling around. Never take a picture without first knowing what your subject is. If you just start snapping photos all around, you likely won't capture much. Instead, be thoughtful about your subject and what you're trying to show. Get close to the subject.

Now think about how to best frame it, or in other words, what elements

Additional Layer

HDR means high dynamic range. This setting on a camera captures a fuller range of light and shadows. It actually takes 3 photos in 3 different lights, one after the other. It then combines the three into one photo.

Additional Layer

Today cameras come with flashes built in. They are bright lights that quickly flash to light up a dark scene so it can be photographed. Photographers used flash powder before camera flashes were invented. They put the explosive powder on a tray and lit it on fire. It produced a flash of light and the picture could be taken while everything was lit up.

Writer's Workshop

Steven Sasson invented the digital camera. Read this interview with him and then write a short biography of his life that highlights his work on digital photography and how it has changed the art of photography.

http://www.megapixel.co.il/english/archive/35884

Additional Layer

Eyes are like windows to the soul. If you can capture a photograph with a clear picture of the light catching someone's eyes, it will be one to keep. Practice with someone you know.

Additional Layer

Along with focusing on the background and foreground to make your subject stand out, you also need to simply avoid the awkward. It's all too easy to snap a photo without noticing that there's a tree growing out of Aunt Sue's head. Or cousin John looks huge because he was standing much closer than everyone else. Or maybe your best friend's leg seems to have disappeared when it's covered by the dog's leg. Pause before you snap a photo, and make sure there's nothing awkward happening. It can usually be fixed easily. If I had moved a foot either direction, my field of flowers photo could have avoided the awkward grass beard I have.

should you include around it in your photo so your subject really stands out? Think of the surrounding scene almost like a picture frame. If it's too busy or distracting, it actually takes away from the focus on the subject. If there's something in the background or foreground that makes your subject look unnatural or strange, that's also distracting. How can you use the scenery to point to your subject? These two pictures were both taken the same day on a mom and daughters vacation we went on. In the first one, the porch of our cottage frames us nicely, leading your eye to the subjects, my sisters and I. In the second one, I was positioned in a field of beautiful flowers, but one distracting tuft of grass becomes the inadvertent subject your eye travels to.

😊 😊 😊 EXPLORATION: Up Close and Personal

Most of the time, photos are more effective if you get close to the subject and on their level. Don't be afraid to get down on the ground or climb up on something if you need to. Change the angle so that your subject is the main focus. Be close enough that details and personality can shine through. Make sure you can see your subject's eyes if possible. In this first picture, Jason is riding a trike and I am standing above him. In the second picture, I sat right on the driveway and got down on his level, then waited until he zoomed over to me before snapping the photo.

☺ ☺ ☺ EXPLORATION: Extreme Close Up

Get really, really close to capture some intricate details of objects.   Use photo editing software to crop the photo to only show the detailed textures and colors of your pictures. Have someone try to guess the items you photographed just from your close up shots.

☺ ☺ ☺ EXPLORATION: Rule of Thirds

If you are thinking about taking a photograph like a painter would think about making a painting, you can make some artistic choices that will set your photo apart. The Rule of Thirds is a trick photographers use to make their photos look more interesting. Instead of placing your subject right in the center of your camera's viewfinder, place it just off of the center, on either the right or left third line. You can do the same thing with up and down placement, putting the subject just above or just below the center line. There's nothing wrong with centering a photo sometimes, but subjects are perfectly centered so often that it becomes boring. To create interest, use the Rule of Thirds instead, and place your subject just off from the center at one of these grid points instead.

☺ ☺ ☺ EXPLORATION: Photograph an Event

For this exploration you need to attend an event. It could be a wedding, a party, a picnic, a family movie night, or a holiday celebration. Sometimes we feel like we have to capture a whole scene all at once or make sure every single person in attendance is in

On The Web

Watch "My Life As An Adventure Photographer" by National Geographic to hear the real life experiences of a National Geographic photographer. https://youtu.be/MYECOURXy5M

Famous Folks

Matthew Brady was an important photojournalist who documented the American Civil War. Learn more.

Famous Folks

Phillippe Kahn is an inventor who was inspired to invent the first camera phone when his daughter was about to be born and he wanted to send her picture to family and friends. He rigged his phone to a camera and sent the first phone picture that was ever taken of his daughter.

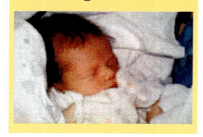

every picture. But those pictures usually lack a clear subject and get boring, because they are all the same. Instead, you will focus on choosing specific subjects that take you through the story of the event.

You will only be allowed to take 6 pictures to tell the story of the event you chose. Think about 6 different subjects that will tell the story. Here is an example of what you might capture at a picnic:

- The picnic basket sitting atop the blanket on the ground
- A close up of someone taking a bite
- Food
- Ants or other visitors
- Someone eyeing a delicious dessert
- People playing on the grass in the sunshine

Without a single photo of the entire picnic, we told the story with pictures in a way that captured the feeling and narrative.

☺ ☺ EXPLORATION: Photojournalist

Become a photojournalist by photographing something and then writing a story or news article about it. Photojournalists utilize all kinds of news stories, from headline events to sports competitions and public interest pieces. You could even decide on an issue that's important to you, like littering or animal abuse, and write an editorial that includes a photograph.

Flood Waters Within Our Walls

A suspect was apprehended yesterday morning while fleeing the scene of the crime. Jason, age three, plugged the sink and left the water running in the upstairs bathroom Sunday morning. A massive flood ensued, soaking the upstairs and downstairs bathrooms, with water trickling through the cabinets, floors, and walls. His sentence would have been far more severe had Mom not been writing a talk on compassion at the time. Jason's previous crimes include spreading flour throughout the house, chugging milk straight out of the jug, and vandalizing his sister's bedroom.

Decide on something newsworthy and take a picture that highlights the event. Write an article to accompany it. This could be a news item in your community, a club or team you participate in, or some family news.

Good photojournalists include pictures that really help tell the story or shed light on the event or issue.

☺ ☺ ☺ EXPLORATION: Photo Scavenger Hunt

Go on a photo scavenger hunt. You can create your own list or use the Photo Scavenger Hunt printable from the arts section of the printables on Layers-of-Learning.com. You will need at least two teams of people. This is a great activity to invite friends for. Each team will have at least one camera and will need to photograph each item on the list, trying to return before the other team does.

For extra fun, have a projector or television set up to a laptop and quickly import the pictures that each team takes, then have a slide show. It's sure to be full of stories and laughs from the scavenger hunt. You can also arrange for a prize for the winning team and goodies for all.

☻ ☻ ☻ EXPLORATION: Creative Perspective

Creative perspective is a fun, modern form of photography that plays with images and tricks your eye. Search online for "creative perspective photography" and peruse some of the pictures. Design your own creative perspective photo shoot in which you capture an image in a creative way. You can pattern it off of one you saw, or come up with your own idea.

Additional Layer

Taking glow in the dark photos can be really fun. Use Christmas lights, glow sticks, or sparklers. If your camera has manual settings, you can experiment with them. Generally, for glowing items you want a high ISO and a low f-Stop.

Famous Folks

Anne Geddes is a masterful photographer who specializes in creative perspective baby portraits. Go explore annegeddes.com and navigate to the gallery to be amazed by her unique baby portraits.

Coming up next . . .

Unit 4-7

Latin America
New England States
Animal Groups
Latin American Art

My ideas for this unit:

Title: _____   **Topic:** _____

_____
_____
_____
_____
_____
_____
_____
_____
_____
_____

Title: _____   **Topic:** _____

_____
_____
_____
_____
_____
_____
_____
_____
_____
_____
_____
_____

Title: _____   **Topic:** _____

_____
_____
_____
_____
_____
_____
_____
_____
_____
_____
_____

Title: _____ **Topic:** _____

_____

_____

_____

_____

_____

_____

_____

_____

_____

_____

Title: _____ **Topic:** _____

_____

_____

_____

_____

_____

_____

_____

_____

_____

_____

_____

Title: _____ **Topic:** _____

_____

_____

_____

_____

_____

_____

_____

_____

_____

_____

_____

Vietnam War Dogs

This is an American soldier with his dog in Vietnam. The dogs were used to sniff out mines and booby traps. Many soldiers became very attached to the dogs and treated them like favorite pets and not just working dogs.

Vietnam War Timeline

1954	**1955**	**1965**	**1964**
North and South Vietnam are split	North Vietnam attacks South Vietnam	U.S. aid to Vietnam has reached $500 million	A U.S. ship in the Gulf of Tonkin is attacked by North Vietnamese ships and sinks one of them, U.S. orders retaliation on North Vietnam
1965	**1968**	**1969**	**1973**
U.S. Marines arrive in Vietnam	Tet Offensive by the North Vietnamese. Military defeat for Vietnamese and moral defeat for Americans	A peak number of 543,500 troops are in Vietnam	Peace accords signed in April by all parties; Americans completely pull out. Fight continues.
1975			
North Vietnamese capture Saigon.			

Vietnam War
1964-1973

China

North Vietnam

Red River

Dien Bien Phu

US Air Raids (1966-1973)

Hanoi

Haiphong

Mining of Haiphong Harbor (1973)

Xam Nua

Gulf of Tonkin Incident (1964)

Laos

Gulf of Tonkin

Vientiane

Mu Gia Pass

Raids on Supply Routes (1965-1973)

Demilitarized Zone

Quang Tri Province (1972)

Khe Sanh (1968)

Tet Offensive (1968)

Invasion of Laos (1971)

Thailand

Mekong River

Ho Chi Minh Trail

Mai Lai

Dak To (1967)

Pleiku (1965)

Bangkok

Cambodia

Invasion of Cambodia (1970)

Central Highlands (1965-1971, 1975)

South Vietnam

Phuoc Long Province (1974-1975)

An Loc (1972)

Xuan Loc (1975)

Saigon

Saigon (1975)

Gulf of Thailand

Mekong Delta (1957)

South China Sea

◇ American Air Base
▢ American Base
✦ American Offensive
✧ North Vietnamese Offensive

Layers of Learning

This is Lieutenant Johnson. He's not wearing any rank insignia so the enemy won't target him. He and his men are pinned down by the Viet Cong as they are trying to escort some mothers and their babies out of the fighting zone. He is carrying a grenade launcher.

Vietnam Diorama Figures

Color the figures. Make a jungle background in a shoe box. Add the figures into your diorama.

Layers of Learning

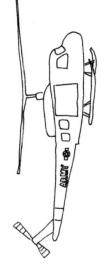

This is a "Huey" helicopter. Officially it is the Bell UH-1 Iroquois. It was the most common helicopter of Vietnam. It was important in medical evacuations.

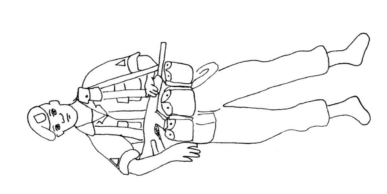

This is Sergeant Kelly. He is a Green Beret, special forces. He's been in Nam for almost a year. He'll be going home soon, but after what he's seen he'll never be the same. He's carrying an M-16 rifle.

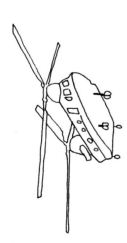

This is the Chinook helicopter. It is fast and can carry heavy loads over long distances. It was used as a troop transport vehicle during Vietnam. It was also famously used to carry heavy gun batteries to the top of remote mountains.

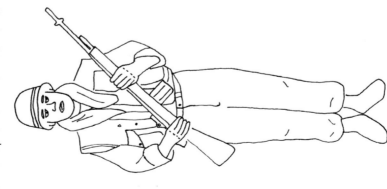

This is Private Harris. He is carrying an M-1 rifle. He has only been in Vietnam for a few weeks. So far his platoon hasn't seen any fighting, but he'll be going up country tomorrow morning.

Atlantic States

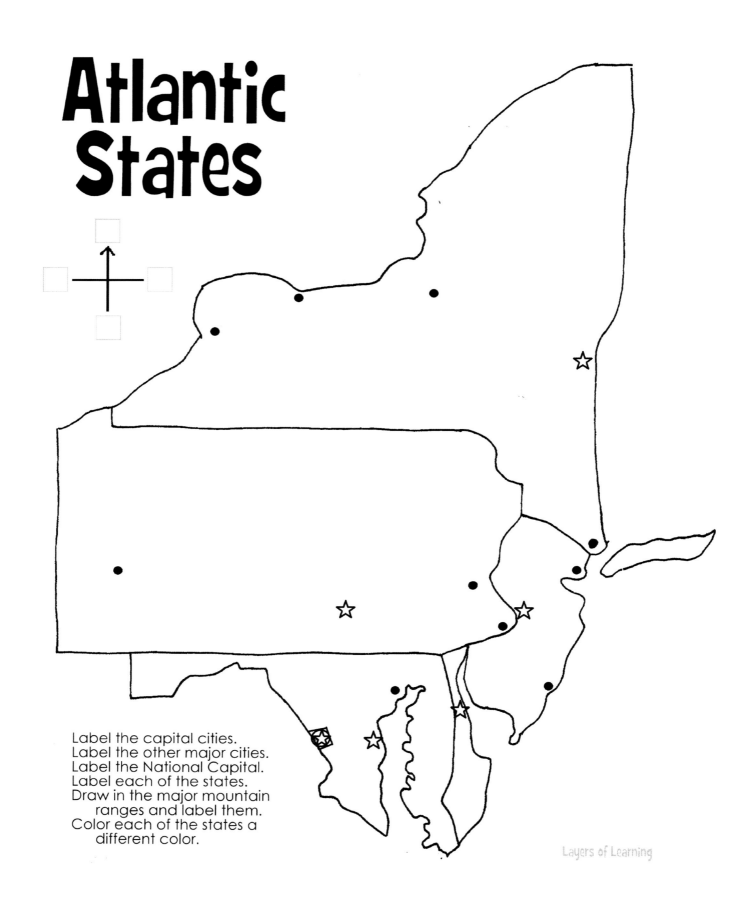

Label the capital cities.
Label the other major cities.
Label the National Capital.
Label each of the states.
Draw in the major mountain
  ranges and label them.
Color each of the states a
  different color.

New York	Pennsylvania	New Jersey
Delaware	Maryland	Albany
Harrisburg	Trenton	Dover
Annapolis		Match the States to the Capitals

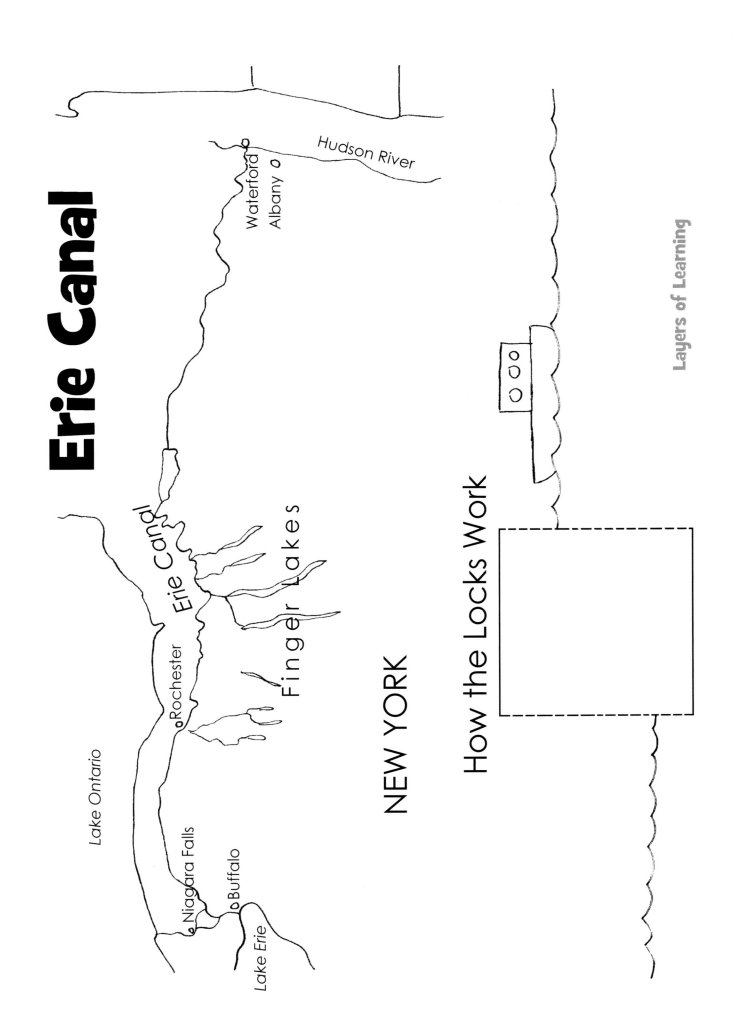

Erie Canal

Hudson River

Waterford
Albany

Lake Ontario

Rochester

Niagara Falls

Buffalo

Lake Erie

Erie Canal

Finger Lakes

NEW YORK

How the Locks Work

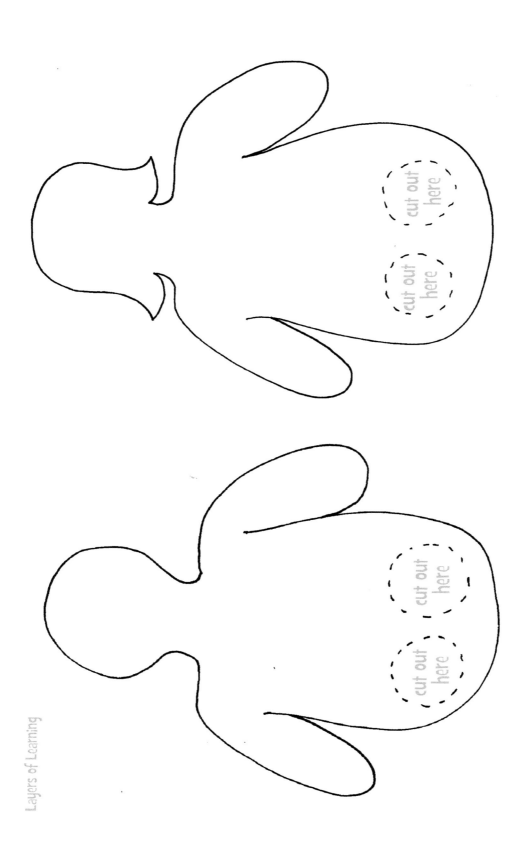

People of the Atlantic States Finger Puppets

cut out here

cut out here

cut out here

cut out here

Atlantic States Baseball Review

1. What is the capital of New York State? Albany

2. Name the river that runs up the western border of Maryland and flows past the city of Washington D.C.. Potomac

3. What is the name of the big island off the eastern coast of New York? Long Island

4. What is the waterway that cuts up through the center of Maryland called? Chesapeake Bay

5. Hershey, Pennsylvania is known for what food? Chocolate

6. In the west, Pennsylvania borders which of the Great Lakes? Lake Erie

7. Which famous waterfall is between Lake Erie and Lake Ontario and the border between New York and Canada? Niagara Falls

8. Which city is the largest in the United States? New York City

9. Land from which state was carved out and given to the federal government to be a capital for the nation? Maryland

10. The Adirondack Mountains are in which state? New York

11. The Hudson River flows past New York City between which two states? New York and New Jersey

12. Dover is the capital of which state? Delaware

13. Only Rhode Island is smaller than this Atlantic State. Delaware

14. Atlantic City, famous for the boardwalk and gambling, is in which state? New Jersey

15. Which ocean do the states of New York, New Jersey, and Delaware border? Atlantic Ocean

16. The largest city in Pennsylvania's name translates to "The City of Brotherly Love." What is the name of this city? Philadelphia

17. What is the name of the capital of Pennsylvania? Harrisburg

18. "Excelsior" means higher and is the motto for which state? New York

19. This city was the first capital of the United States of America. Philadelphia

20. The capital of New Jersey was once captured by George Washington during the Revolutionary War. What is it called? Trenton

21. Maryland's capital is also the site of the Navy's academy. What is the name of Maryland's capital? Annapolis

22. What is the name of the bay between Delaware and New Jersey? Delaware Bay

23. The long narrow lakes in upstate New York were cut by glaciers. What are these lakes called? Finger Lakes

24. In which state is the Erie canal located? New York

25. This city was once the capital of the United States and was where George Washington was inaugurated president. New York

26. The climate in the Atlantic States region is temperate and fairly wet. What kind of habitat does it have? Deciduous forest

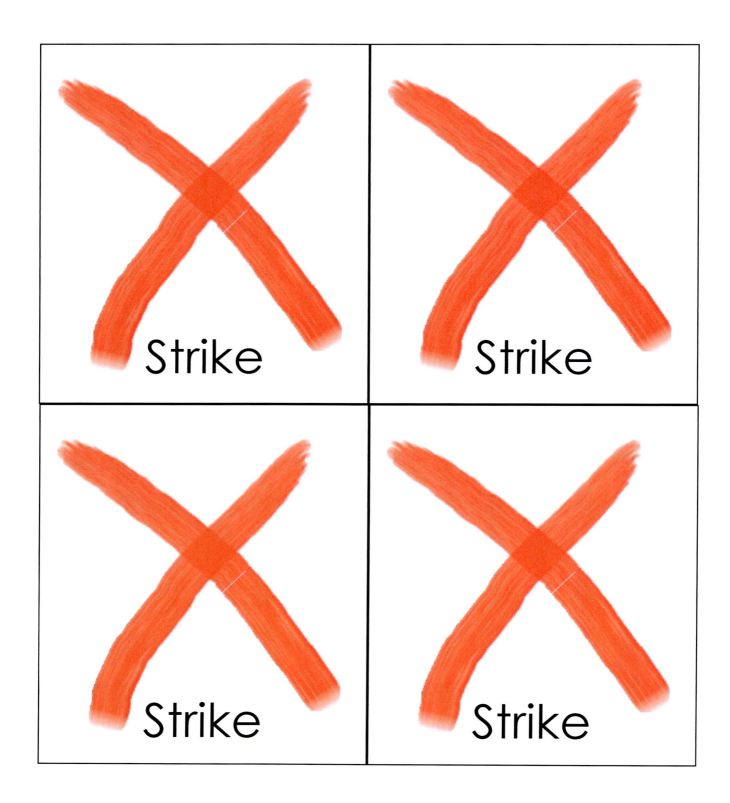

Philadelphia
Phillies

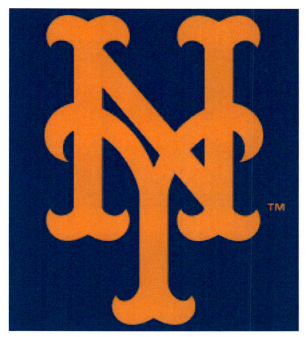

New York Mets

Baltimore
Orioles

New York
Yankees

1869 Ernst Haekel coins the term "ecology"

Ecology Timeline

Color the pictures on this page and the next. Then cut them apart with their descriptions. Paste them in order on other paper along a timeline.

1972 Acid rain effects on lakes is discovered and studied by Harold Harvey

1970s James Lovelock's idea of Gaia is formulated; the whole earth is one living entity and will ensure its own survival even if humans destroy themselves

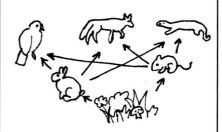

1927 Charles Elton makes the concept of food chains and webs part of ecology

1852 Robert Angus Smith connects acid rain to air pollution

Late 1700s Antoine Lavoisier, a chemist, discovers oxygen and carbon and their importance to living things

1940s Ruth Patrick studies interdependence of organisms, particularly freshwater ecosystems. She develops methods to measure the health of a stream.

1933 Aldo Leopold writes Game Management beginning the discipline of wildlife management

1915 Ecological Society of America is founded

1900 Henry Chandler Cowles studies ecological succession

1950s People first become aware of the harmful effects of pollution on ecological systems and on people

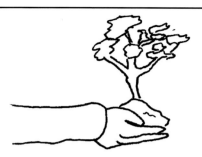

1978 Conservation biology is established as a discipline focusing on environmental management

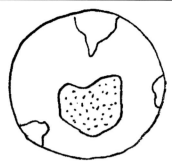

1980s Scientists discover a hole in the ozone layer over Antarctica

1935 Arthur Tinsley defines ecosystem

1980s Water pollution seriously reduced due to new sewage treatment practices

1875 Eduard Seuss defines the biosphere

Late 1800s Animal camouflage studied and described

1879 Symbiosis is first described

1935 The Dust Bowl crisis refocuses ecology on practical land usage practices

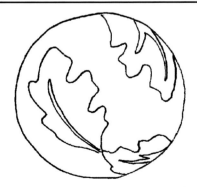

1951 Nature Conservancy is founded

1953 Eugene Odum and Howard Odum write the first ecology textbook and ecology becomes a university course

1980s Air pollution is reduced in cities as unleaded gas and catalytic converters are use din autos

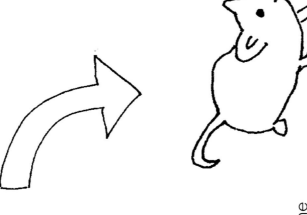

Food Chain

The grasshopper eats leaves. The mouse eats the grasshopper. The cat eats the mouse. And the wolf eats the cat. So the population of grasshoppers affects the wolf. Sometimes population problems among animals low on the food chain can have big effects on the animals at the top of the food chain.

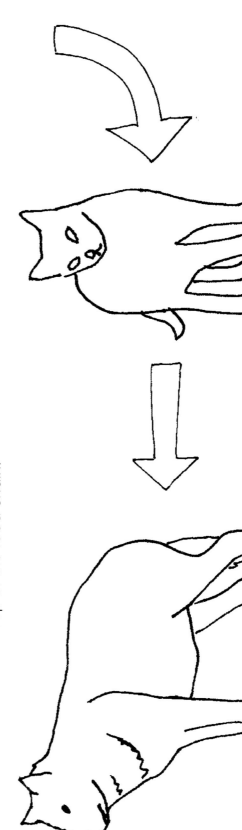

mouse	grasshopper	fox	cat
worm	robin	owl	deer
cow	snake	mushrooms	rabbit
wolf	vulture	grasses and seeds	hawk

Complete-A-Chain

Fill in the blanks in the food chains below.
Who eats who?

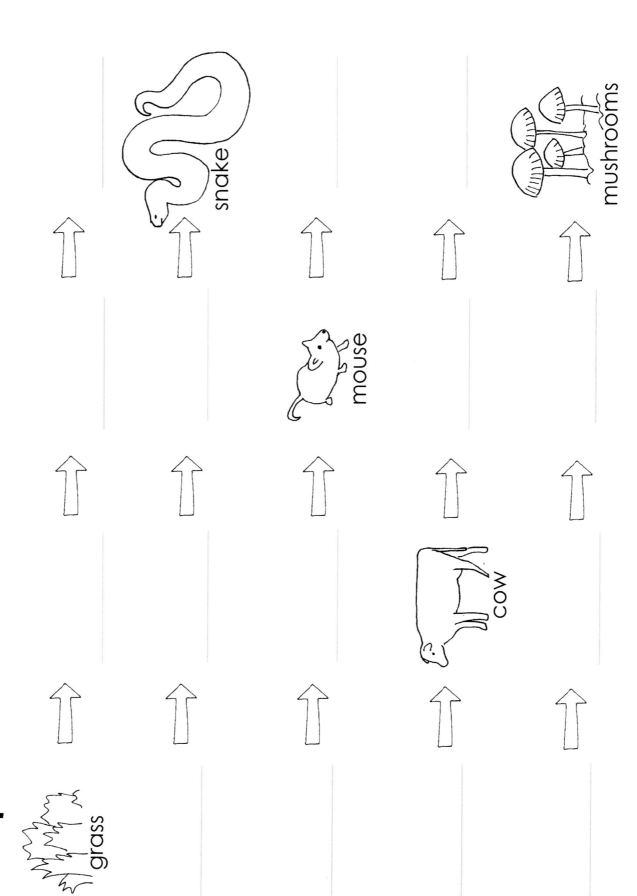

grass

cow

mouse

snake

mushrooms

Food Web

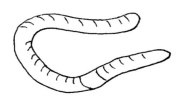

Connect the animals with arrows pointing in the direction the food moves. You will create a web of interactions between animals. How many animals want to eat the grasshopper? What is the role of the vulture?

Ecological Pyramid

Cut apart the tags at the bottom of the page. Paste them on in the correct positions on the ecological pyramid. Draw pictures of animals that belong on each level of the pyramid. Think about the sizes of these populations in the wild. How does population size and reproduction rate relate to the ecological pyramid?

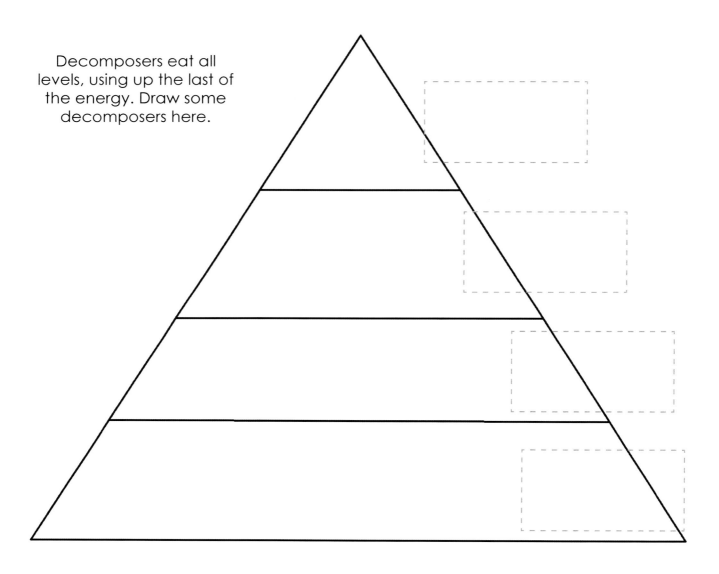

Decomposers eat all levels, using up the last of the energy. Draw some decomposers here.

| Secondary Consumers | Producers (Plants) | Primary Consumers | Tertiary Consumers |

Label A Camera

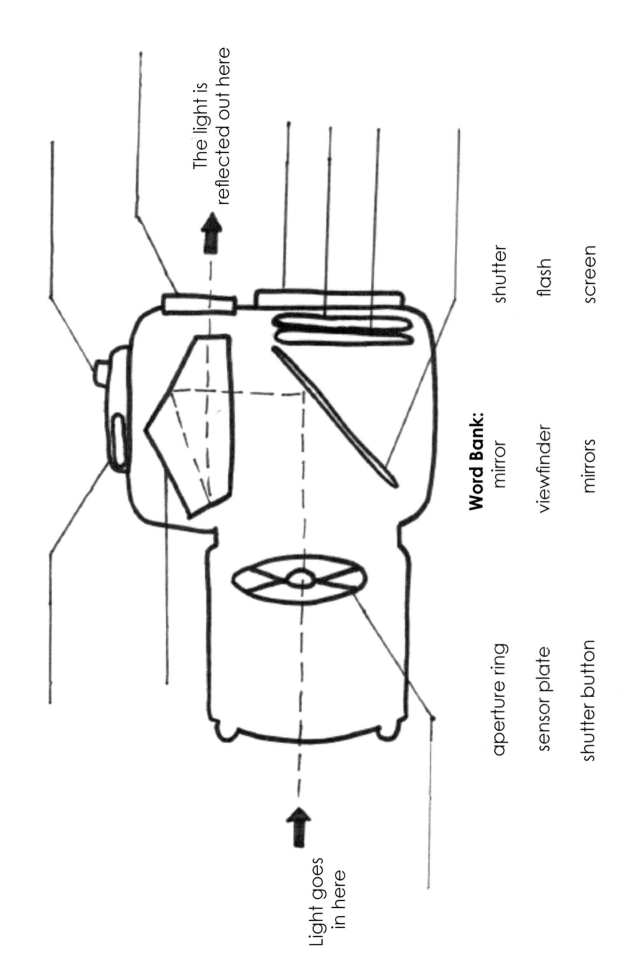

The light is reflected out here

Light goes in here

Word Bank:

mirror	shutter
viewfinder	flash
mirrors	screen
aperture ring	
sensor plate	
shutter button	

Pixelated Picture

Use each small box as a pixel, or one dot of the picture. Each small box must be filled in with one solid color. Create your own pixelated picture of a simple object. Real pixels are very, very small, but as they all combine together, they form one big picture. Here are a few ideas for pictures you could make: a strawberry, a heart, a flower, a dolphin or fish, a turtle, a spider, a tree, a castle, Pac-Man, an owl, a dinosaur, a bear, a butterfly, or a bird.

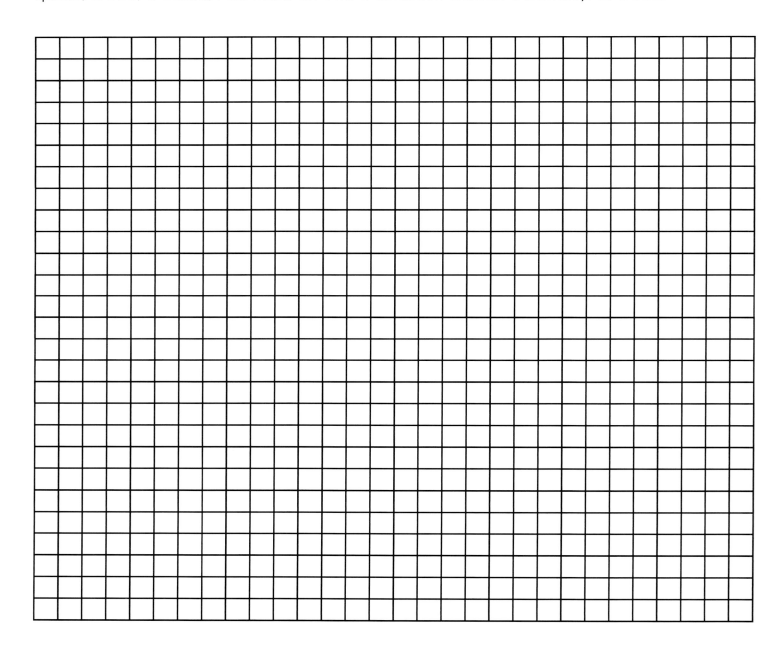

Ansel Adams

His
Life

His
Nose

His
Interests

Photo-
grapher

Nature &
National
Parks

Environ-
mentalist

About the Authors

Karen & Michelle . . .
Mothers, sisters, teachers, women who are passionate
about educating kids.
We are dedicated to lifelong learning.

Karen, a mother of four, who has homeschooled her kids for more than
eight years with her husband, Bob, has a bachelor's degree in child development with an emphasis in education. She lives in Idaho, gardens,
teaches piano, and plays an excruciating number of board games with
her kids. Karen is our resident arts expert and English guru {most necessary
as Michelle regularly and carelessly mangles the English language and
occasionally steps over the bounds of polite society}.

Michelle and her husband, Cameron, have homeschooled their six boys
for more than a decade. Michelle earned a bachelors in biology, making
her the resident science expert, though she is mocked by her friends for
being the Botanist with the Black Thumb of Death. She also is the go-to for
history and government. She believes in staying up late, hot chocolate,
and a no whining policy. We both pitch in on geography, in case you
were wondering.

Visit our constantly updated blog for tons of free ideas,
free printables, and more cool stuff for sale:
www.Layers-of-Learning.com

Made in the USA
Middletown, DE
04 April 2025